1

ROBERT MCNAIR WILSON

PROMISE TO PAY

An Inquiry Into The Modern Magic

Called High Finance

ⓞMNIA VERITAS

ROBERT MCNAIR WILSON

PROMISE TO PAY

An Inquiry Into The Modern Magic

Called High Finance

First Published in 1934

Published by Omnia Veritas Ltd

𝒪MNIA VERITAS

www.omnia-veritas.com

TABLE OF CONTENTS

In the civilised world there are enough raw materials, machinery, labour and scientific knowledge to satisfy the needs of all the inhabitants.

Poverty and hunger exist because people have not enough money to buy all the output of modern civilisation at a fair price to the producers.

When there is a shortage of anything the most obvious remedy is to create some more and there is no real difficulty in creating more money. **PROMISE TO PAY** shows how this should be done when money is backed by goods and services.

The creation of money should be in the hands of the State or Head of Government and not in the hands of private banking. The state would issue sufficient money to enable the buying power to keep pace with production.

Paper money issued by banks is not real money but "Promise to Pay" money and the amount in circulation bears little relation to the amount of goods and services available.

When there is less money than goods, people go short of food and clothes. When there is more money than goods prices rise and people pay more and more for less and less.

PREFACE

Next to the weather, finance is now the most talked about subject in the world. But discussion remains difficult owing to the confusion which exists in many minds about the nature of money. In the following pages an attempt has been made to describe the money system so that its principles may be grasped easily by anyone above the age of sixteen years.

I wish to thank my friend C. Featherstone Hammond for the great help he has given me.

R. McNair Wilson.

INTRODUCTION

I t is a crime in this country to coin money or to print banknotes. The reason is two-fold. If a man counterfeits money and spends it, he has gotten goods without working for them, and has taken by stealth a little of the riches of his neighbours.

The last crime is more heinous than the first as can be understood by consideration of a simple instance. Let us suppose that we have taken our places at an auction sale. There are few buyers and prices, in consequence, are low. Then a stranger enters the salesroom and begins to bid. The auctioneer immediately gets higher prices. The newcomer's money has made everything in the sale room more valuable and has, correspondingly, reduced the value of all the money on offer.

By bringing his money to market and using it there to buy goods, the counterfeiter raises the price of goods, and so lowers the value of money. He enriches sellers at the expense of buyers by increasing demand; for money is most valuable when it is least plentiful. If it was possible for a counterfeiter to double the number of £1 notes in use, each £1 note, of those existing before the counterfeiter began his operations, would buy only half the quantity of goods which it bought before. In other words each one pound note would soon be worth only 10s [50 pence - ed].

Counterfeiters, therefore, are thieves in the respect that they slip their hands into other men's pockets and take away a part of the value of other men's money. All have to pay for the goods which these rogues are getting. Like brigands, indeed, they force honest folk to give them tribute. The theft, so secret and hidden that none is aware of it, is not less real than the picking of a pocket or the emptying of a safe.

It follows that any creation of new money, no matter by whom made, diminishes the value of the money already in use. The owners of money already in use suffer loss, when new money is put into circulation, without knowing how this loss has occurred. All that they are aware of is that the price of goods has risen and that, in consequence, their money buys less. In fact they have been compelled, without their knowing it, to pay a kind of "invisible tax".

Who gets the benefit of this invisible tax? In the case of the issue of false money the benefit, obviously, goes to the counterfeiter. In the case of the issue of good money, the person or persons issuing the good money is enriched.

In former times new, good money was issued only by the King and his Government. It was used to pay for public works such as the upkeep of the army and navy and the service of public health and education. Thus, what the owners of money had lost, when the new money was created, came back to them, later, in the form of a reduction of taxation. The "invisible tax" took the place of the visible one. But since, in modern days, Governments have everywhere surrendered to private individuals the right to create what is in effect new money, the benefit gained by the creators of the new money is no longer returned to the public. The private creators of new money, like the counterfeiters, keep the benefits to themselves and thus profit at the expense of all their neighbours including the King and his Government.

Worse still, the surrender to private individuals of the power of creating new money has given these private individuals the power to change the prices of goods, or in other words, to alter the price-level. The more new money they create, as has been seen, the dearer will goods become.

In these circumstances ordinary citizens owe it to themselves and to one another to obtain some understanding about the way in which money is now created by private individuals and about the uses which these private individuals make of the money created by them.

I   CONFIDENCE

From very early times people have taken their money to strong-rooms and vaults because of their fear of burglars. In most towns some citizen built such a strong-room and set up in business as the keeper of his neighbours' gold and silver. He offered security and charged a small fee for it.

He used, further, to supply his clients with receipts for their money. If you put £100 in gold into his strong-room he gave you an IOU for £100.

When you came back to take the money away the IOU was destroyed. The IOU in other words was a promise-to-pay signed by the owner of the strong-room.

The particular owner of a strong-room, with whom we are now concerned, happened to be an observant man. He noticed after a time, that very little of the gold and silver which had been entrusted to him was ever taken away again. People brought hundreds of pounds; but they seldom wanted to remove more than a few pounds at a time. He noticed, further, that people whom he had not seen before came to his strong-room with IOUs and demanded money for them. These people explained that they had taken the IOUs in payment for goods supplied or in payment of debt.

"Bur my IOUs are not money," he protested. "Why should you take them instead of money?"

"Because we know that you've got the money here in your strong-room."

"How can you know that?"

"We trust you. Those who have taken your promises-to-pay have always got their money when they asked for it."

"So you are using my promises-to-pay instead of money? Just as if they were real money?"

"Why not? It's much safer and more convenient to use a slip of paper than to carry round bags of gold or silver. We all know you in this town. Your name on a promise-to-pay is as good as gold. The shopkeepers take your IOUs. One can buy food and clothes - anything at all - with them. Why bother to draw out gold or silver unless one is going on a journey into towns where your name is not known?"

The owner of the strong-room thought long and deeply about this conversation. It was true; his promises-to-pay were being used instead of money by the whole town. Farmers took them in exchange for their beasts and crops at the markets; shopkeepers took them; the doctor and the lawyer and even the tax-collector took them. Very well then, they were money, seeing that money is anything for which people will give goods or services or which they will accept in payment of debt. The owner of the strong-room opened the door of his vault and looked at the bags of gold and silver on his shelves. Suppose that, by chance or ill-luck, half of that money got lost, nobody would be a penny the wiser or a penny the worse off. There would still be enough, far more than enough, left to meet all the demands for gold or silver that were ever likely to be made. The promises-to-pay would go on circulating just the same; people would take them just as eagerly as before.

The owner began to study his ledgers. He found that, on average, only one-tenth part of the gold and silver held by him was ever asked for. If a client had put £100 in the strong-room, the odds were that, during any year, that client would not draw out more than £10. The other £90 would lie idle on the shelf from one year's end to the other. That meant, as he saw, that if he lost even as much as nine-tenths of all the gold and silver entrusted to him, he would still be in a position to meet every claim for gold or silver that was likely to be made upon him. His promises-to-pay would be just as highly valued as before and just as readily accepted.

For all those who wanted gold or silver could be supplied with it the moment they presented their IOUs.

He had, at this time, some £10,000 in gold and silver in his strong-room and there were, therefore, promises-to-pay to the value of £10,000 in the hands of his clients. Why not increase the number of promises-to-pay to £100,000? The idea seemed so wild, so preposterous and so dangerous that, at first, he put it away from him. How could he sleep easily in his bed if he knew that people held IOUs for £100,000 in his strong-room?

Could he be sure that his promises-to-pay would go on circulating instead of real money? Might not all his clients descend on him, one day, in a body, with their IOUs in their hands, demanding gold and silver in exchange for them?

But that mood of panic passed. Day followed day without bringing any change in the habits of his fellow townsmen. A few of them came to take away small sums of money. These were people about to travel into regions where his name was not known and where, therefore, his IOUs would not be accepted, or people in need of pocket money or people obtaining coin with which to pay servants' wages.

The great mass of the population never entered his door. They went on paying and receiving in the shops and markets his IOUs exactly as they had always done. And still his ledger bore witness that, on an average, only one-tenth of the quantity of gold and silver in his strong-room was ever asked for.

Timidly, therefore, and with great caution, our owner of the strong-room went into the business of lending promises to pay what he did not possess. Having found a client who was short of cash, he offered him £100 worth of IOUs on condition that the loan was repaid by a certain day and that it carried, meanwhile, interest at 5 per cent. As a guarantee of good faith the borrower handed over the title deeds of his house, saying that, if he failed to repay the IOUs the lender could sell the house and so recoup himself.

This guarantee given by the borrower caused the lender a pang of conscience. For he was well aware that he had lent no money at all buy merely a promise to pay money. The fact that people would give goods for these IOUs did not in the least alter the fact that they were IOUs and nothing more - IOUs moreover, which lacked a backing of gold and silver.

He had created these IOUs out of nothing; why should he receive interest on them? Again, since they were going to play the part and fulfil the functions of true money, was he not guilty of creating money in the manner of a counterfeiter? Had his strong-room not become a kind of private mint?

These uneasy questions troubled him for a time but when the loan was repaid, with interest, his scruples vanished. After all, he told himself, he had not created any new money. All that he had created were promises to pay money. What had really taken place was a fair exchange of debts. He had borrowed the title deeds of his client's house; his client had borrowed the title deeds of £100. As his client continued to live in the house, his client also was obtaining interest on what he had lent.

But conscience continued to prick the banker now and again. The house, as he knew, had cost his client hard work. It had been earned; whereas the IOUs for £100 had cost nothing. They had been created out of nothing, invented by a stroke of the pen. Worse still, they played the part of money, exactly like false coin of forged banknotes. They added, therefore, to the total quantity of buying-power and so, by raising prices, had made all the rest of the money in the town a little less valuable.

Every other citizen had thus been forced to contribute his or her share of the newly-created "money". He, the lender of the IOUs, in other words, had stolen from all his fellow citizens, and had obtained interest upon the stolen "money".

But the system had worked well and conferred benefits on others. Nobody so much as suspected that a robbery had taken place. On the contrary, everybody was delighted. The borrower had been able to develop a new line of his business; there was more trade in the town; it had been possible to give employment to some idle hands. The lender noted all this and proceeded, quietly, to find new borrowers for his IOUs until he had lent £100,000 worth of them and was, consequently, in receipt of an income from interest of £5,000 a year. As soon, moreover, as any loan was paid back he made haste to relend it.

The town now had IOUs for £100,000 in its shops and markets. Prices began to rise sharply and everyone with anything to sell made a profit. As a consequence there was a boom in business and large quantities of goods were manufactured. The farmers cultivated new acres and more food came on the market. But this rise in prices went on only while the owner of the strong-room was engaged in making his loans of IOUs. He noticed that each time he stopped lending prices stopped rising. And each time prices stopped rising business in the town fell away. The hope of making bigger and bigger profits on a rising market had been taken away.

He began to find himself, now, in a difficulty. Because he had lent the whole of the £100,000 (in the form of IOUs) he had set out to lend. He visited his strong-room again. His shelves were no longer crowded with bags of gold and silver. On the contrary, they were nearly empty. His ledger showed him that the amount of gold and silver which he took in each day only just equalled the amount of gold and silver which he had to pay out to the people who wanted to change his IOUs for actual coin.

He gave the matter further careful consideration. Every one of his IOUs, those he had lent as well as those he had given as receipts for gold and silver, were promises to pay gold and silver. Consequently, any of the borrowers of his IOUs could ask for gold and silver in exchange for them.

All these borrowers, indeed, as he very well knew, supposed that it was gold and silver which they were borrowing. They had taken IOUs simply for convenience sake because, like their fellow townsmen, they believed that the lender was good for the money. If the slightest suspicion got about that all the IOUs could not, instantly, be transformed into gold and silver - but he put that terrible thought away from him. He had always had enough coin on his shelves to meet the demands made upon him.

Everybody who had presented an IOU at his counter had instantly obtained gold or silver for it.

But if he went on lending IOUs above the £100,000 worth things might be different. His original calculation had proved in practice to be sound. It was true that people used IOUs in preference to gold and silver and that the amount of gold and silver asked for was, roughly, about one-tenth of the amount of IOUs asked for. He had started a banking business.

People paid in his IOUs mixed up with gold and silver coins just as if the one was as good as the other. They carried away the same mixture, coins for payments outside of the town and IOUs for payment to their fellow townsmen. Confidence in him was complete. But it depended upon the apparent interchangeability of the metal and the paper.

That must, therefore, be maintained at all costs. In no circumstances could he dare to create IOUs in excess of ten times his holding of gold and silver. He must, therefore, now that he had created the full amount which his holding of the precious metals allowed him to create, draw in his horns and refuse to lend more.

Instead, therefore, of welcoming new borrowers, as had been his custom while he was spreading out his IOUs, he began to discourage them: he could not, he said, see his way to make further loans. He had already gone as far as he felt able to go. The buoyancy at once went out of the market. Those who had bought in the hope of selling at higher prices found themselves disappointed; those who had produced goods to sell at higher prices began to grow uneasy.

The owner of the strong-room shared to some extent in this anxiety. For every loan of his IOUs made by him he had taken some security, a mortgage on a house, or a herd of cattle or a stock of wine or jewellery or silver plate. The prices of all these things were weakening. Would the householder, the farmer, the wine merchant, the owner of the jewellery or plate be able to repay? And if not, would he, the banker, be able to get back his IOUs when he sold the securities?

Another fear came to disturb his sleep. While he was lending and while, in consequence, prices were rising, money had been changing hands with great speed. Both coins and IOUs had passed quickly from buyer to seller and from seller back to buyer again. The borrower had spent as fast as possible in opening a new factory and rushing new goods on to the rising markets. This spending had paid for buildings and materials.

Thus IOUs had been brought back at once to the bank by builders and tanners and smiths and other master-tradesmen, who, in their turn, had spent them on wages. They had poured swiftly through the bakers' and butchers' and greengrocers' shops and these retailers had also fetched them back to the bank and then, later, drawn them to pay their bills to the millers and farmers and market gardeners and so on. Almost every day new accounts had been opened with the bank, each of them consisting of statements of the number of IOUs held by the person owning the account.

The banker knew what these statements really represented. He knew, for example, that the £100 worth of IOUs which he had lent to the glovemaker had been spent by that man in paying £80 to the tanner, £10 to the furrier and £5 each to the horner and the threadmaker. The banker's account stated that he, the tanner, possessed £80. The furrier's account stated that he, the furrier, possessed £10, and so on. But what these people actually possessed were his, the banker's, IOUs. Suppose that the fall in prices alarmed all these good people to the extent of making them wish to possess gold and silver. If that happened an army of clients would appear one morning at the door of the bank, each of them with his hands full of IOUs and each of them demanding coin, hard cash, red gold. The banker, tossing on his bed, resolved that not only must he stop lending; he must shorten sail. He was confirmed in this resolution when he saw that his IOUs were no longer passing so quickly from hand to hand. The slowing down of business had caused a corresponding slowing down in the rate of circulation of money. People were not spending. On the contrary, they were allowing their IOUs to lie in the bank. Thus, the quantity of "money" in the markets was diminishing; there were fewer and fewer bidders at the sales.

The banker, in these anxious circumstances, bethought him of his loan of £100 to the glovemaker. He called that man into his private office and sat down opposite to him:

"I have no wish, of course," he said, "to embarrass you in the conduct of your business; but I do feel that, in present circumstances, it might be well if you could see your way to pay off your loan."

He spoke in the quiet, firm tones of a man who is asking regretfully for his own. The glovemaker flushed and wiped his brow.

"You hold my house," he said, "as security for the loan. It's worth £500 if it's worth a penny."

"Oh, my dear sir, things in this world unhappily are worth only what they will fetch."

"What, do you suggest you haven't got good cover?"

"Not at all. But the loan has been outstanding for six months. Banking, you know, is not exactly money-lending. We are the handmaidens of industry... "

"What can it matter to you if you have security?" The banker shook his head.

"It's difficult to explain. Finance, I find, is a closed book to the majority of men. Well, each to his trade." He paused. "What about a mortgage on your house? You could borrow enough to repay my loan."

The glovemaker went away. But he did not take the banker's advice.

Instead, he called on a shopkeeper who had bought a consignment of his gloves worth £100 and urged that he must be paid at once. The shopkeeper had no option but to advise the tanner, the furrier, the horner and the threadmaker, all of whom had accounts with his shop, that they must immediately pay off their debts.

Next morning the banker found tanner, furrier, horner and threadmaker standing behind his counter. Each drew out his little stock of money - in the form of IOUs - and closed his account. The sums withdrawn paid the shopkeeper, who paid the glovemaker, who repaid his loan to the banker, who wiped the promises-to-pay out of existence with a stroke of his pen.

The banker could now look at his ledger with less anxious eyes (because this process of calling in loans had not, of course, been confined to one client only). He saw that he no longer owed anything to the tanner, or the furrier or the horner or the threadmaker! And he was no longer in any danger, by reason of the possible failure and default of the glove maker, of not getting back all the IOUs he had lent to that man. In all he had called up, let us say, half his former loans of IOUs; there were now only £50,000 of these outstanding. In other words his holding of gold and silver amounted to one-fifth instead of one-tenth of his promises-to-pay.

He was glad that he had, thus, reduced his risk when, soon afterwards, some of the more timid among his clients began to change their IOUs into coin. He ventured to ask one of these timid folk why he was taking such a course.

"Because we feel that, with so many people losing their money, you cannot have escaped losses yourself."

While this scene was in progress an old man entered the bank. The banker, with a start, recognised one of his original depositors, a man who had placed £4,000 in gold in his strong-room. The old man came to the counter and put down IOUs to the value of £4,000.

"I want my money, please."

The banker's face became expressionless. He raised his hand as if to wipe his brow but immediately lowered it again.

"Certainly."

There were a number of people in the bank. They moved nearer, craning their necks. The banker signed to his clerk and they went down together into the vault. A few minutes later they came back carrying the bags of gold. They placed the bags on the counter. The old man opened one of the bags and poured some of its contents into his hand. The bright gold met his eyes genially. He sighed, bent down and then stood erect. He turned to the other people in the bank.

"There you are," he said. "There's my money. Who says now that our banker hasn't got the gold and silver to meet his IOUs?" He turned to the banker.

"I heard a rumour that you'd had losses like the rest of us. I knew it wasn't true, mind you; but I thought I'd just put you to the test."

He made a gesture with his long arms.

"Take it back where it came from," he cried. "Your IOUs are good enough for me."

II ECONOMIC LAW

The banker was able to congratulate himself now on the steps he had taken. His IOUs had never stood higher in the regard of his fellow citizens. He was able, in the cases in which he felt justified in renewing a loan, to ask for a higher rate of interest., as much as 8 per cent. Thus, although his loans were fewer in number, his income, all things considered, remained wonderfully steady.

His case, indeed, was in striking contrast to that of his fellow citizens. As the result of the withdrawal of one-half of the IOUs - that is to say of one-half of their accustomed buying power - they found themselves with tumbling markets and slumping prices. The mass of goods created during the boom had become largely unsaleable except at ruinous prices. Firms were closing down and discharging their work-people, or close cutting wages to the bone in an attempt to keep going. There were riots which had to be put down with force. There was hunger in the middle of overflowing plenty. There was bankruptcy of once-prosperous and honoured families. Masters were horrified to find that their men resisted a reduction of wages which, as these men ought to have seen, had become urgently necessary; men stood aghast at the "savagery" of masters who desired, it appeared, to take the bread out of their children's mouths.

Nobody, meanwhile, could account for the disaster.

What had happened? Why had prices fallen? What blight had descended on their wonderful prosperity? In their deep perplexity men turned to the banker. He, at any rate, had ridden out the storm. In a world where everything was falling in ruins he stood like a rock.

The banker received a deputation of the chief citizens and entered with them into a consultation about the sickness of the community. The Mayor, who was a businessman, expressed the view that there had been a gross over-production of goods. But one of the Aldermen, a Labour leader, called this opinion in question.

"How can there be over-production when half the town is starving, without decent clothes or boots?" the Alderman asked.

The Mayor could not answer him. A doctor in the deputation proposed the inauguration of relief-works for the unemployed. But the Mayor shook his head.

"The town is in debt to our friend the banker," he said. "We could scarcely ask for a new loan at present."

"There are the rates."

"My dear doctor, we are finding the greatest difficulty in collecting the rates."

They all turned to the banker. He waited for silence and then addressed them.

"Need I say, Gentlemen," he began, "that I have

given the most anxious thought to the sad plight in which we all find ourselves? Believe me that, if I speak plainly, I do so only from a sense of duty. In my opinion there has been over-production. There has also been over-spending by the public authority. You built a swimming bath, a new school, a play-pond."

The banker watched the Mayor as he spoke. That official looked guilty.

"These are luxuries, gentlemen, luxuries; delightful and most proper if one can afford them. You see, when the public authority sets an example of... lavishness, plain citizens are likely to lose their heads. Men dream dreams. They build too many houses, too many factories, too many workshops. A great mass of goods is thrown upon the market. Has anyone asked himself: 'Where is the money to come from to buy all these delightful things?'"

The banker glanced about him. Nobody spoke.

"I address you," he went on, "as the custodian of the savings of my fellow citizens. These hard-earned savings have been entrusted to my care and I regard the trust as a sacred one. My first duty, clearly, is towards my clients. Very well, then, I say that further expenditure by the municipality would certainly not be justified. Where is the money to come from? Capital, as you know, is derived from savings, it is produced by saving, by thrift, by the exercise of frugality and honesty. Are these savings, the provision men and women have made for their old age, to be risked in enterprises which, in any case, are unlikely to achieve their object? Gentlemen, I have a different plan to propose."

The banker leaned across the table.

"We, too," he said, "must save. We must build up more capital resources. We must cut down every item of expenditure, public and private, which cannot be justified. If we do that we shall be able to pay the interest on our debt."

The Alderman: "To you."

"Certainly to me, as the custodian of the savings of your fellow townsmen. Let me add, Gentlemen, that I believe that many of our public services are over-staffed... "

"Would you take the loaf off the table when the children are sitting down to tea?" the Alderman exclaimed.

A growl of anger went round the room. The Mayor called the Alderman to order.

"There's no escaping economic law," the Mayor said.

"Ah," the banker cried, "that's it. Economic law. Inexorable economic law. We are all the servants of economic law. Yes, my friend, we must deny ourselves, tighten our belts... "

"Why should we tighten our belts when there's been

over-production?" "We have been living beyond our means."

"What do you mean by that?"

"The swimming bath, the new school... "

"We built them. How can it help anybody if we don't use them?" "They can be sold."

"Only at ruinous sacrifice."

"My dear sir, the value of anything is what it will fetch. If we have lived beyond our means, can we go on enjoying luxuries which we cannot afford?"

"I say that it's ridiculous to tighten your belt in the middle of overflowing plenty."

"Our prosperity was fictitious."

"What, bread isn't bread, is it? Leather isn't leather? Cloth isn't cloth? We've got them, I tell you; why can't we make use of them? Look at the unemployed. How can you say a town is poor when it has hundreds of idle craftsmen and masses of raw material? Is an army poor when it has great numbers of reserves? Does a general surrender before he has called up his reserves? And while his supply services are bulging with goods?

Surely it's madness in such circumstances to talk about cutting down? Why not use what we've got? Why not set our people to work?"

The banker shook his head.

"Where is the money to come from?" he asked, and added: "What would you say to me if you brought me one of my IOUs only to find that I did not possess the means of cashing it? Ask yourself that question. I could create IOUs in unlimited quantities - by a stroke of the pen. Would you accept them in payment? Would you wish to feel that you had entrusted the fruit of your frugality and hard work to such scraps of paper? Why are my promises-to-pay valuable? Because I can redeem them in gold and silver. If you insist on my issuing IOUs which cannot be redeemed what will happen? Prices may rise for a time. What then? Wages also will rise. That, my dear sir, is what a banker calls inflation."

The last word came in tones which conveyed an impression of finality. The Mayor nodded vigorously.

"Oh, no, no," he cried. "No inflation please. No inflation on any account whatever. I return thanks every day that, whatever else may be weak, our financial system is sound. Sound as a bell." He wiped his brow. "There's no doubt that the banker is right. We have been living above our means. Both profits and wages have been too high, Our prosperity was unreal, fictitious, a bubble. The bubble has burst. Well, we must be men. We must tighten our belts and pay our debts no matter at what price. Those of us who are more happily situated must try to help our less fortunate brethren."

He wiped his brow again. A faint smile appeared on his lips.

"Meanwhile," he declared, "I know that I shall be expressing all our thoughts when I say that we feel grateful to our banker for his courage and for the clear and definite manner in which he has explained our trouble and prescribed the appropriate remedy. Our banker, as many of us know, has gone to the extreme limit of safety in order to help us. He has done what he could to temper the wind to the shorn lamb. But there is a limit, the limit set by economic law. No prudent man, no honest man, can go beyond that. I, for one, wish to say that I am thankful that our banker has shown himself both prudent and honest, a worthy custodian of our savings. Our hearts may be troubled; they are troubled. But at least we can say: 'There has been no inflation'."

The banker spent that evening over his ledger. He saw that he had become possessed of a very large number of business houses and shops, because the owners, who had owed him IOUs, had gone bankrupt in the slump. He reached the conclusion that if, in the near future, he could see his way to extending his loans once more, all this property would inevitably rise in value. He decided to hold the property against that happier day.

His conscience had ceased to trouble him. But he couldn't help thinking that whereas he had spread out his loans in the first instance, and so raised prices, every buyer had been compelled to pay him tribute, now, when he had called in his loans and so caused prices to fall, tribute had come to him from the sellers. It was a case, evidently, of heads I win, tails you lose. His earlier fears seemed absurd in the light of what had actually happened. He had begun operations with £10,000, all of which belonged to other people. But here he was now the owner of half the houses and businesses in the town, and therefore of a large proportion even of the gold and silver in his own vaults. Whereas formerly his income had been derived solely from the small fees he charged for keeping other people's money in his strong-room it was derived now from a long list of Investments, from rents and from the profits of business. He was the richest man in the town and also the most powerful. And every one of his fellow citizens held him in honour.

III   THE "CREDIT CYCLE"

Further consideration showed the banker that he had been able to exert so great an effect upon the lives of his fellow townsmen because he had given them buying power, in the form of his promises-to-pay, when they had no need of it and had taken that buying power away at the moment when their need of it was greatest. At the time when he had begun to lend his IOUs there had not been a great quantity of goods in the town's markets. There had not, therefore, been great need of money to distribute these goods. The sudden flooding of the empty markets with money - a true inflation - had, in consequence, sent prices soaring up and made it worth everybody's while to produce more goods. Soon the markets had become glutted with goods, so that large quantities of money were needed to distribute them. The sudden draining away of the money, in these circumstances, had necessarily brought all prices down with a thud. His IOUs had given him control of the price-level.

But he comforted himself with the idea that, even if money had never been invented something of the kind would probably have happened. After all, it was human nature to produce to excess any article for which a brisk demand seemed to exist. And excessive supply is bound, sooner or later to extinguish demand and so to leave producers with their goods in their hands. He made that point to a friend who had offered some criticism of his methods; his friend shook his head, objecting:

"Demand was not extinguished in this town. The town is still full of hungry men and women and children."

"They have no money."

"We're not talking about money. You said that what has happened here would have happened if money had never been invented. I say that it would not have happened. It was your loans which caused the boom;

it was the withdrawal of your loans which caused the slump. There's all the difference in the world between a population which has satisfied its needs and has, after its needs have been satisfied, a surplus which it cannot use, and a population that is starving among plenty."

The banker did not pursue the subject. He assured himself that, in any case, his loans had had the effect of developing the town and all its industries. They had acted like a stream of water in a desert.

"You'll admit that we've got a move on. Look at the expansion. The progress!"

"And the misery."

The methods adopted by the banker were, naturally, adopted very soon by other keepers of strong-rooms in other parts of the country and, indeed, throughout the world, with the result that there was witnessed a sudden and violent expansion of production and then an equally sudden and violent contraction. This alternating boom and slump became a permanent feature of the whole world's trade and was called "The Trade Cycle", or "The Credit Cycle". What was not generally realised about this "credit cycle" was that the bankers were making profits both ways, by compelling buyers to pay them tribute during the booms and by compelling sellers to pay them tribute during the slumps - and all this by means of their loans or promises-to-pay what none of them possessed. Our banker delivered an address to his fellow townsmen on "The Credit Cycle".

"This movement of prices up and down," he declared, "is inherent in human nature. It belongs, too, to the nature of things as well as to the nature of men. Look at the seasons. Out of winter darkness emerges the sunlight of spring. That is transformed soon into the glory and happiness of summer. But all too soon the days begin to draw in. Comes the fall of the leaf and then, once more, winter darkness. Believe me, my friends, in the pessimism which now infects our spirits we see only a reflection of Nature herself. But let us lift up our hearts:

'If winter comes can spring be far behind?'" The good man pointed to the skies.

"What is it," he asked, "which causes a revival in trade? Surely it is confidence. Confidence in ourselves. Confidence in our fellows.

Confidence in the future. Because we feel confidence returning to our spirits we begin to plan, to look ahead, to devise new means of production. Such a change of heart, believe me, cannot be produced artificially by any banker. Can a banker, by some act of financial wizardry, induce farmers to expect harvests at seed time? There is a time to sow and there is a time to reap. How can a banker lend when no man wishes to borrow? How can he refuse to lend when substantial and credit-worthy borrowers approach him? Never forget that a banker's first duty is towards his clients, the honest and frugal folk who have entrusted to him the savings of their lifetime. Would you have him risk these savings in loans that no man desires? Would you have him make use of your savings to attempt to change the laws of Nature, to try to sow in the time of reaping? Again, would you hold him back from affording you the chance to help yourself and all your fellows by granting aid to the masters of the harvest when their fields are white and their trees heavy with fruit? It is confidence which begins a boom, my friends; and it is lack of confidence which brings it to an end. There is no financial conjuring trick, believe me, which can change by an iota that law of nature, that economic law, that inexorable economic law."

"A banker, indeed, can only follow where wisdom and prudence lead. If he does not expand his loans when there is a genuine need of them, he will be failing in his trust: if he does not contract his loans when confidence has begun to ebb away he will be wanting in common sense."

In private, however, the banker was less happy than he had been. A cloud of a most unlooked-for kind had begun to darken his horizon. This cloud was in the form of another banker, living in the capital city of the country, who had developed the business of lending his IOUs to the merchants engaged in trade with foreign countries. The International Banker was concerned, above everything else, to see that the volume of foreign trade was well maintained, that is to say that a brisk demand for his loans continued to exist. He had noticed that when booms occurred in the home market the volume of foreign trade tended to diminish because people were able to buy their own goods and did not wish to export them. He was anxious, therefore, to prevent the Home Bankers from lending too much in the home markets.

When Our Banker understood what was afoot he became very angry and declared that he would tolerate no interference with the conduct of his business. He would lend his IOUs when and to whom he chose and he would withdraw them only at such times as seemed good to him. He defied the International Banker to do his worst.

But he was uneasy, nevertheless. For in his heart of hearts he knew that the promises-to-pay in which he dealt were promises he could not possibly fulfil if any large number of his clients asked for their money at the same time. He decided that, in future, he must be more careful than ever before to "keep his position liquid", that is to say to invent smaller quantities of his IOUs and to lend them only to borrowers of the most trustworthy substantial kind.

The International Banker, however, had another plan to propose. Why not, he suggested, bury the hatchet and co-operate instead of quarrelling?

"I am in need, often", he said "of sums of money to lend to shippers and merchants. I am prepared to borrow for short periods of time, a night or a weekend even, so that your money will always be within your reach if you want it. Why not lend me the IOUs for which, at the moment, you cannot find good borrowers in your own town?"

The banker thought over this proposition; and the more he thought about it the better he liked it. It was true he often had difficulty in making a new loan immediately. Good, sound borrowers were none too easy to find, especially in times of slump. Consequently he was often in the position of having IOUs to lend and not being able to lend them - a most distressing state of affairs seeing that his unlent promises were earning no interest.

The International Banker offered him what was, evidently, a way out of his difficulty. He could hand over to the International Banker all his unlent IOUs with the comfortable assurance that the loans were for very short periods of time. It would be a matter of hours only to call up any of these loans, so that if a good borrower came along he could always accommodate him by withdrawing IOUs from the International Banker.

He accepted the offer therefore and began to re-organise his system of lending. He was still in possession of gold and silver to the amount of £10,000. But in future he would not lend the whole of these promises in his own town. He would divide his loans into short loans and long ones. He would lend, say,

£20,000 to the International Banker and £80,000 to his fellow townsmen. When business was very bad in the town he might even lend £40,000 or £50,000 to the International Banker and only £50,000 or £60,000 to the town. In booms, on the contrary, his loans to the town would be increased and his loans to the International Banker diminished. In that way all his IOUs would be kept at work earning interest and he would be in a position to shorten sail overnight if need be. He would be holding a substantial part of his IOUs in a very "liquid" state.

The plan worked exceedingly well and the banker found his income Increased by it. When he thought that conditions in the town were ripe for a new boom - when the old stocks of goods had been sold off at rubbish prices and the bankrupt businesses disposed of to fresh owners - he withdrew some of his IOUs from the International Banker and put them, cautiously, into circulation at home. Prices at home then began to rise. People saw a chance of profit and production was speeded up. More and more of his IOUs were now withdrawn from the International Banker - who only paid about 2 per cent - and entrusted to fellow townsmen who paid 5 or 6 per cent. Then, when the new goods which the boom had created began to come on the markets he took in sail again by calling up some of his loans to his fellow townsmen and returning these IOUs to the International Banker until such time as the slump had developed and so prepared the way for another boom.

Since rates of interest rose while he was withdrawing his loans from the town and did not fall again until the slump had touched bottom he obtained an income from his own clients which varied very little. In addition, he got another, smaller, income from the International Banker. The International Banker, on his side, obtained IOUs over and above those which he was able to create for himself, just when he had most need of them - that is to say during the periods of slump when manufacturers, who could not sell their wares at home, were shipping them out of the country into foreign markets and so were in need of the International Banker's services.

"What I do," the International Banker explained, "is to lend IOUs to merchants who have cargoes to export or import. I take the cargoes as security for my loans. The merchants, of course, pay me interest."

Our banker understood very well what this meant. The International Banker, like himself, was engaged in inventing promises-to-pay. He was lending these at interest and thus obtaining tribute from his clients for nothing. The danger he had to fear was that his clients might demand the fulfilment of the promises - might demand that is to say gold or silver in exchange for the IOUs.

This demand for gold was likely to occur when outgoing cargoes did not balance, and so pay for, incoming cargoes, because, in that case the difference would have to be paid in gold. Bills of exchange, in other words, which are the IOUs of international trade, would no longer serve as the means of payment. The International Banker would be forced to honour his signature his signature upon these bills by giving gold for them. As he, too, was lending promises-to-pay ten times the amount of gold in his possession he could not do this to any great extent.

Our banker realised all the dangers involved in such a system. But he was growing accustomed to dangers. He fixed his thoughts on his own business and began to interest himself in the development of railways. He lent considerable sums of his IOUs for the building of lines to his home town. A boom in consequence developed and very soon the whole of his available IOUs were in the hands of home borrowers.

As a consequence of this flooding of the home market with money, large numbers of people became possessed of buying power. More goods, therefore, were sold at home and the export trade began to languish. Very soon there were not enough exports to balance, and so pay for, imports.

What had been foreseen now occurred. The International Banker found himself faced by demands that he should fulfil his promises to pay gold, and became panic-stricken lest the demands should exceed his holding of that metal. When the drain of gold had continued for some days he lost his nerve. What was he to do? The answer seemed to be that he must shut his doors. He stopped lending abruptly and tried to call up as many of his loans as possible. Foreign trade, in consequence, came to a standstill.

The effect was to throw goods designed for export on to the home market and so to cause prices at home to break. At the first sign of this danger all the Home

Bankers also began to call up their loans. The boom had been violent; the slump was equally violent. Our banker gazed at his ledger with terrified eyes. Hundreds of accounts had been opened with him. Would he be able to call up his loans before the panic which was spreading over the whole country brought his clients to his door? People who owned gold were hoarding it. He demanded his IOUs from every borrower and so compelled borrowers in their turn to put pressure on their debtors. But day by day, in spite of these drastic methods, his holding of gold leaked away. He began to sell the houses and shops of borrowers who could not repay their loans. The slump was so widespread that neither houses nor shops fetched even moderately good prices. They had to be sold at a ruinous sacrifice. He watched his counter. All his clients who had credit balances seemed to want gold. Everybody wanted gold. His shelves were growing emptier and emptier and still there were thousands of claims, thousands of his promises-to-pay, outstanding against him.

In his despair he rushed off to the capital city. Would the great National Bank help him? He would pay anything, anything at all, for some gold and silver to tide him over the crisis. The National Bank, when he reached it, was besieged by a crowd of Home Bankers all of whom were as frantic as himself. He was told that there was no gold to be had. The public was hoarding it.

He had to return home. He proceeded to sell everything that he possessed, all the wealth that had come to him in other days, his horses, his country house, his plate - for within the limits of the system he was an honest man. Thanks to these extreme sacrifices he was able for another week, to keep his doors open. But at the end of that time his vault was empty and the demands for gold had not ceased. He made up his mind, as he lay abed, that he would not open his doors on the morrow.

He did not sleep. His morning letters were brought to him. One of them announced the declaration by the Government of a Moratorium for debt and the issue, by the National Bank, of notes to replace the vanished gold. He need not pay out another gold or silver coin. He was saved.

ROBERT MCNAIR WILSON

IV   THE BALANCE OF TRADE

He explained to his clients next morning that the crisis was over.

"What has happened," he said, "is that a gold famine was produced by the inconsiderate action of a few selfish hoarders. Though we possessed claims on gold we could not obtain the metal. And so the Government has stepped in and said that, till things right themselves, the notes it is about to issue through the National Bank will be counted as gold. They will be the same as gold. They will be legal tender. I hope to have a supply of these notes today when I shall begin at once to pay them out to those who feel doubtful about the value of my IOUs."

As soon as people knew that the Government was standing in behind the banks they ceased to feel frightened. Within a few weeks our banker had his gold back again on his shelves and had begun, once more, to build up his fortune. He had not done so badly. If he had sold many of his assets at a heavy loss, he had many more assets in his hands for which he could count on getting reasonable prices. His losses, moreover, were losses not of money but of promises to pay it. These promises had cost him nothing. Now that he had the gold back on his shelves he could begin to invent more of them. The boom was over; the town wallowed in the succeeding slump. People with credit balances on his books, therefore, would have to withdraw them in order to pay their debts and since many of these debts were owed to borrowers from himself he would soon be able to cancel a substantial number of his IOUs.

He set his house in order and then lent the IOUs he did not wish to use at home to the International Banker, who had also, thanks to the fall in prices, got out of his difficulties. The goods which could no longer be sold at a profit at home were being rushed into foreign markets. Exports were rising high enough to balance and pay for imports. The demands for gold to be sent abroad were no longer being made.

But the International Banker, nevertheless, was very much shaken. He and his colleagues called a meeting of the Home Bankers in the Capital City.

"Gentlemen," said the International Banker, "you must now see that this state of affairs cannot be allowed to continue. Look what has happened. There was a chance of making big profits in railway construction. What did you all do? You rushed in, headlong, with your IOUs and lent everything you could lend in the hope of getting high rates of interest. Up soared prices in consequence; up went wages. There was so much buying power in the home market that nobody had any wish to export - even supposing that it had been possible, in view of the high wages and therefore of the high costs of production, to sell anything outside of the country.

"What was the result? Not enough exports to balance and pay for imports. A demand by foreigners with claims against this country for payments in gold.

Like yourselves we, the International Bankers, lend our IOUs to the extent of ten times our holding of gold. The demands upon us were far greater than our means of meeting these demands. We had to stop lending. We had to call up every available loan. Foreign trade came to a standstill. That reacted back on you because it threw onto the home market the goods which could no longer be shipped abroad. Home prices also fell. You know the rest."

The speaker paused for a moment. When he saw that he had produced the effect he wanted, he added:

"Those of us who have weathered the storm were saved by the action of the Government in declaring the moratorium and giving leave to issue notes. But the Government is profoundly uneasy and the public is panic-stricken. If this sort of thing happens again it is as likely as not that the Government will take the banking system our of our hands. We will be turned into mere agents, forbidden to create private promises-to-pay and compelled to handle instead the Government's promises. There will be small profit for any of us in that arrangement. So it follows, evidently, that we must add safeguards to our system, such safeguards as will make it impossible for any boom in the country to reach such dimensions as to interfere seriously with the export trade. I have to propose... "

Here the International Banker assumed almost a threatening expression.

"I have to propose that, in future, when a golden coin leaves this country a National Bank note to the value of that coin shall be removed from circulation - in other words that buying power to the amount of the departing gold shall be taken from the home market. Such a withdrawal of buying power as you know, will at once produce a fall in prices and bring the boom to an end before it has become a danger to all of us."

Our banker rose and glanced about him uneasily.

"You are asking us," he said, "to consent to an arrangement which places us wholly in the hands of yourself and your colleagues - of International Finance. And not us only. Our clients as well. The whole nation."

"No, sir."

"Yes, sir. Because it comes to this: if you, the International Bankers, choose to make large loans of your IOUs to foreigners, and if, in consequence, gold leaves this country... "

"Excuse me, but our business is to finance trade."

"Do you deny that you make loans to foreigners? To foreign governments?"

The International Banker was silent for a moment.

"Money," he said, "must find its level. It must be allowed to flow into those markets where it can promote the largest possible amounts of wealth."

"That means where it can earn the highest rates of

interest compatible with safety," our banker exclaimed.

"Well?"

"Your loans to foreigners may easily upset the exchange so that gold must flow out of this country. Suppose for example that you lend £1,000,000 to the Greek Government to build a railway and suppose, further, that the Germans are producing rails more cheaply than we can produce them. The Greeks will buy their railway in Germany."

"Certainly."

"And you, the lenders to the Greeks, will therefore have to pay the Germans."

"Yes."

"In marks."

"Of course. Pounds would be no use to the Germans." "You will have to buy your marks with pounds?"

The International Banker nodded. He shrugged his shoulders.

"What you are going to say," he remarked, "is that, if we buy marks with pounds, the marks will grow dearer and the pounds will grow cheaper - on the Foreign Exchange Market. Of course they will. The more the demand the higher the price." He held up his hand to silence our banker who wanted to speak. "I'll finish your complaint for you," he exclaimed. "You were going to say that if marks become too dear in terms of pounds, it will be cheaper to use the pounds to buy gold in the first instance and then to use the gold to buy marks. I admit that, too. Gold will leave the country in these circumstances."

"And when gold leaves, if you get your way, notes will be taken out of circulation here at home."

"Quite so. That is my proposal." "And prices will fall?"

"Yes, and wages also. Then we shall be able to make railways as cheaply as the Germans, more cheaply perhaps. When that happens foreigners will buy in this country, and we shall not need to send our gold away."

"It means," the Home Banker said, "that you can play one country off against another; that you can force the workpeople in all countries to accept the same wages as the lowest-paid workpeople in any country; that in consequence, you can prevent any country from retaining enough buying power to buy its own goods and so can force any country to export its goods in competition with all other countries; it means bitter competition between nations for foreign markets, armaments and preparations for war - perhaps in the end war itself. We, the Home Bankers, will be powerless to resist you because, if you send gold out of the country, we shall automatically be compelled to shorten sail, to call up loans - no banker can expand his loans on a falling market."

"My dear sir," the International Banker exclaimed, "you can lend abroad just as well as we can. If you have IOUs to spare you can invest them with us or you can invest them with foreigners. It will be all to your advantage because you will be getting the highest rates of interest which the world offers and, at the same time, compelling the people at home here, to produce more cheaply and so make better borrowers of themselves. We're money-lenders, remember, not philanthropists. What's more, we're all in the same boat. What we have to secure is that we can create our IOUs and that, having created them, we can lend them at the highest obtainable rate of interest. We can only be sure of doing that if the act of taking money out of a country compels that country to produce more cheaply. Our IOUs must find their level. And they must not, on any account, be replaced without our consent in the countries from which we have withdrawn them. The reason why governments must never be allowed to interfere with our operations is that the interests of governments are nearly always opposed to our interests. Government always wants to avoid a fall of prices and wages and a rise of unemployment and, therefore, a government is always tempted to create money to replace the IOUs we have taken away."

V   FOREIGN EXCHANGE

A few days later, at a more intimate gathering, the International Banker explained his view with greater clearness.

"The sap and marrow of this business of money-lending," he declared, "is a moveable price-level and hence a moveable wage-level. You Home Bankers know perfectly well that if prices or wages were fixed or pegged in any way, if they were even moderately stable, you would soon be out of business. Imagine such a state of affairs. Farmers would know, roughly, what they were likely to get for their crops; manufacturers would know what they could expect to obtain for their goods. They could all, therefore, arrange their businesses with confidence. They could set so much aside for rent, so much for wages, so much for machinery. And they could do this with a good assurance that the sale of their products would enable them, year after year, to pay expenses and put a profit in their pockets. ***Very soon they would get out of debt.***"

He paused and fixed his eyes on our banker, who was listening uneasily.

"What would be your position then?" he asked our banker. "Your loans paid off; your hands full of your IOUs. To whom could you lend these IOUs? All around you prosperous people, people with credit balances on your books; and no means available any longer for making these people wish to borrow."

"Why not?"

"Why not? My dear sir, I am supposing that the price-level, or, since it comes almost to the same thing, the wage-level, has been fixed or stabilized by the Government. If you withdraw your loans, and prices, in consequence, begin to fall, the Government will step in and, by creating money itself, will raise prices again. If you make too many loans and prices, in consequence, begin to rise, the Government will step in and, by taxation, or some other device, withdraw money from the markets and so lower prices again. Buyers and sellers, therefore, will be assured of their markets and will have nothing to worry about except popular taste and the competition of other buyers and sellers. All the competent producers, that is to say all the good borrowers as things now stand, will, as I have said, get out of debt and acquire their own capital. You will not be able to lend your IOUs. Since you are money-lenders and nothing else you will not have any means of livelihood except the commissions you may earn by looking after other men's wealth. We shall be back to the old position of keepers of strong-rooms. We shall be clerks, accountants, cashiers - without influence and without power."

He paused again. Our banker frowned.

"Possibly," our banker said, "that might occur if the price-level, or the wage-level, really was pegged by

Government. But who today is thinking of fixing the price-level or the wage-level? An odd crank here and there, perhaps; nobody pays any attention to them. Everybody, on the contrary, is firmly convinced that what must, at all costs, be kept fixed, is the rate of exchange between our money and foreign monies. and you know that if the rate of foreign exchange is fixed, neither the price-level nor the wage-level can possibly be fixed as well. What you are trying to make us believe is that, unless we, the Home Bankers, give you the power to make us shorten sail and call up our loans whenever it suits you, all our businesses will be ruined."

"Quite so. That is exactly what I am trying to make you believe. And it happens, I may add, to be true. Suppose, for a moment, that you go on as you have been doing. Suppose, for a moment, that such a person as an international banker exists nowhere on earth. Suppose that this country is absolutely self-contained, isolated, shut up within itself so that nobody ever wishes to go outside of it. And suppose, further, that you go on lending your IOUs in the future exactly as you have done in the past. What is going to happen?"

Our banker shrugged his shoulders.

"Very much what has happened before, I suppose," he said.

"You think that, do you? You think that boom will go on succeeding slump and slump boom for ever and ever, while you continue to make money both ways? You think that when your neighbours are poor you will be able to lend them your IOUs and that, when they have grown rich, you will be able, by withdrawing these IOUs, to seize their wealth and make them poor again so that, once more, they will be eager to borrow from you? You think that they will go on, from generation to generation, playing the part of a flock of sheep, growing new coats of wool for you to clip? For that's what it comes to. I can assure you that you're very much mistaken. I'll tell you what, on the contrary, will happen."

The International Banker lit a cigar and leaned back in his chair.

"This is what will happen," he said. "For a time, a few years possibly, you will be allowed to get away with it. That will be so because your fellow townsmen will still be ignorant about what is going on. After a time, however, when they have suffered one or two slumps, they will begin to interest themselves in money matters. Committees of Inquiry and probably Government Commissions also will be appointed. And these Committees and Commissions will have as their chief object the support of the price-level because everybody, of course, will be aware that it was the fall in prices which was the immediate cause of the slump and so of the distress and bankruptcy and unemployment which are attending it.

Students of this subject will explain that prices depend on the amount of buying power in the market and that, consequently, if buying power is kept up, prices will remain steady. They will explain, further, that buying power and wages are very nearly the same thing. 'Pay higher wages,' they will say, 'and prices will rise.'"

"There will be employers of labour on the Committee or Commission and they will at once become very angry and ask how a man can pay higher wages when prices are falling. For a while there will be a wrangle about this. One set of people will declare:

"'*Wages are buying power; raise wages and prices must rise.*'

"Another set, the employers who have to pay the wages, will answer:

"*'Prices have fallen although we did not reduce wages. How can we be sure, therefore, that if we raise wages prices will rise?'*

"In other words does the wage-level decide and determine the price-level or does the price-level decide and determine the wage-level? We all know how that argument goes. But what you Home Bankers do not seem to realise is that anybody who cares to study the subject must reach the conclusion, on the facts available, that wages, as things are today, always follow prices and never lead them. It is when prices rise that the clamour for higher wages begins and the higher the rise of prices the louder the clamour. In the same way, employers never try to cut wages until the prices of their goods have begun to fall. You may say that this is a natural order and you may try to show that it is over-production on the one hand which brings about the fall in prices, and depletion of stocks, on the other, which causes prices to rise. But I warn you that you will not be believed for very long.

"Why will you not be believed? Because there will be before the eyes of your fellow townsmen, daily, the spectacle of hunger and want in the middle of plenty. The word 'over-production' is unconvincing in such circumstances, and so, too, is the word 'under-consumption'. Everybody will see that what, in fact, is lacking is *money*.

"At once you will be faced with the question: 'Why not let the Government print more notes and distribute them?' You will then be compelled to argue that money created in that fashion cannot be sound money and must ultimately do more harm than good. Think of all the difficulties into which such an argument is sure to lead you. For what, in fact, will you be saying? That gold and silver alone are real money and that money which cannot be converted or changed, at the will of the holder, into gold and silver is unsafe and unsound. Think what that contention really amounts to."

The International Banker paused and leaned forward.

"A government," he went on, "built a theatre and staged a play. But because it was generally believed that the tickets for the theatre ought to be printed on pieces of gold, the government did not, itself, issue any tickets. Instead it applied to the only man in the country who possessed any gold and asked him to undertake the issue of tickets.

"This man, naturally, drove a hard bargain. He soon found that people did not like carrying heavy golden tickets about with them and so supplied, instead, paper tickets each of which bore the words:

'I promise to pay the bearer on demand a golden ticket.'

"The scheme worked very well except that only enough tickets to fill the Stalls were issued, so that the rest of the House remained permanently empty, although large numbers of people wanted to buy the vacant seats. In these circumstances the Government approached the issuer of the tickets:

"'Could you not,' they said, issue enough tickets to fill the house?' "He shook his head.

"'My tickets,' he said, 'are IOUs for golden tickets.'

"He said this with great emphasis. Because, in fact, and unbeknown to the Government, he had already issued ten times as many IOUs as he had golden tickets in his safe. He was afraid to issue any more IOUs in case, for any reason, people suddenly began to want golden tickets instead of paper ones. At the same time he was determined that the Government should not find out that paper tickets, which had no golden tickets behind them, served quite well their purposes of filling the seats in the theatre. So when the Government asked, timidly, if it mattered whether or not paper tickets could be changed into golden tickets he flew into a great rage.

"'What!' he cried, 'you want me to print paper tickets without a backing of gold. Are you mad? How can a ticket that cannot be changed into gold give any satisfaction to its holder? How can its holder possibly enjoy your play? How can he be expected to see and hear like a man whose ticket can be changed into gold?'

"So violent and threatening did the issuer of the tickets become that at first the Government was terrified. No doubt he knew more than they did. But after a time a few members of the Cabinet, who regretted deeply the empty seats in the theatre, ventured to approach him again.

"'Surely,' they said, 'the value of the ticket resides not in the material of which it is made or into which it can be changed, but in the theatre and the play.'

"'You want to inflate, do you?' the issuer of the tickets shouted. 'To issue tickets that cannot be changed into gold, let me tell you, is to inflate.'

"'No, sir. We want to fill the theatre. To use the accommodation we have provided for our fellow citizens. Surely real inflation would be issuing more tickets than there were seats? So long as we have empty seats we can safely issue tickets against them?'

"'There you are. Unsound tickets. Tickets that cannot be changed into gold. May the public be protected from such men as you! Could you enjoy a play if you felt, all the time, that your ticket was nothing but a piece of dirty paper? I ask you that.'

"'We should have obtained our seats.'

"'Seats! What are seats when you have bought them with worthless paper? Can a man sit easily on a seat of that sort?'

"'My dear sir, our theatre is very well appointed. The

seating accommodation is excellent in every way. Besides, you know, one gives up one's ticket before one takes one's seat.'

"'That makes no difference.'

"Suddenly the issuer of the tickets changed his ground.

"'How can you be sure,' he asked, 'that if your tickets cannot be changed into gold, you will not print too many of them - so many that there will be no seats for half the holders?'

"'We know the number of seats in the theatre.'

"'That's no safeguard. You're politicians, are you not? Politicians cannot be trusted with tickets. They always print too many. Look at Germany.'

"'We need not print too many.'

"'You always do. Always. Always. Always.'

"The issuer of the tickets shouted himself hoarse.

"'Are we to keep the theatre half empty for ever?' the members of the Cabinet asked, 'simply because of the possibility that too many tickets might conceivably be printed.'

"They left the issuer of the tickets and devoted themselves to a study of his methods. They found, very soon, that he was doing himself exactly what he refused to allow them to do - namely, issuing many times more paper tickets than he had gold with which to redeem them. It did not take them long to see that the reason why he was able to do this was that very few people ever wanted to have their paper tickets changed into golden tickets. So long as people could get seats they were quite content."

The International Banker paused. He wiped his brow.

"You may preach yourselves hoarse in trying to convince governments that money that cannot be converted into gold is useless or dangerous.

Governments will find out that your own IOUs are an example of this useless and dangerous kind of money. And once they make that discovery they will take away your power to issue IOUs at all. They will provide their own money so that the goods which have been produced may be distributed and used."

"But surely," our banker cried, "you don't deny that over-production is inherent in human nature? When men see a profit they rush to take it. It is this confidence which makes a boom and it is lack of this confidence... "

The International Banker interrupted him with a gesture of impatience.

"Keep that stuff," he snapped, "for your public meetings. Ask yourself if you would listen to it after a sharp fall in prices had driven you into the bankruptcy court. What you'd be concerned about in that case would be to find a remedy - to discover some means of preventing prices from rushing up or tumbling down. And you would find a remedy because the remedy, once you begin to look for it, is staring you in the face. Prices rise when people are given money to spend; they fall when the money is taken away.

The remedy, therefore, is to maintain a constant relationship between the quantity of money and the quantity of goods. Nobody knows better than you how easily that can be done. Remember that our method of inventing Promises-to-pay is no longer a secret. Everybody knows that an IOU is not gold and that the number of IOUs exceeds the amount of gold and silver in your vaults. What you can do the Government can do also."

"The Government does not possess gold and silver."

"What! My dear sir, the Government possesses the power to impose taxation. And it can demand that the taxes shall be paid in gold and silver. How long could you stand up to a demand of that sort?"

The International Banker waved his hand.

"Believe me," he added, "one or other of the Commissions or Committees would propose a fixed or regulated price-level. Why, look at the books and papers written by the currency-cranks, as we choose to call them. There are a hundred and one schemes in these books and papers, but each of the hundred and one contains the same bed-rock demand - namely that prices shall be controlled. That is the real meaning of the price-index scheme, of the 'rubber' or 'commodity money' scheme, of the schemes for public works in times of trade depression, of the schemes for raising wages, of the Social Credit scheme. All these reformers are concerned, first and foremost, to counteract our power to raise or lower the price-level. They want to give the proper conditions in which he can get out of debt and stay out of debt. They want, in other words, to put an end to money-lending.

"Now it is obvious that if money-lending comes to an end we come to an end with it. Our business therefore is to see that this country, and the whole world, is kept full of good borrowers and that these good borrowers are not allowed to become capitalists of independent means, able to finance their own undertakings. We have to fix our burden of debt on their shoulders in such a way that it can never be shaken off. The true secret of money-lending is to lend in such a way that the debt can never be repaid except by contracting a new debt. That can only be accomplished if the price-level remains free to rise or fall as we may determine. Clearly, therefore, some element which can be relied upon to bewilder the minds of producers and reformers is necessary to the safety, and indeed to the existence, of our system. What is that element?"

The International Banker leaned forward again in his big armchair.

"It is," he declared, "the element of foreign trade. Once the element of foreign trade is firmly fixed in people's minds there can be no more talk about fixing the price-level. Do not forget that a stable price-level means a stable level of wages. Wages and costs, let me repeat, are nearly the same thing. If our wage-level is higher than that of, say, Germany, how can we hope to sell our goods in foreign markets against German goods? We must therefore keep wages down. But if we keep wages down we are also keeping buying-power down. Hence we shall have a surplus of goods always, which cannot possibly be sold in the home market. These goods must go into foreign markets or else remain at home to depress further the level of prices. Every producer will live in fear of these surplus goods.

Every producer will desire to see these surplus goods sold abroad so that they may not remain at home to destroy his market. Every producer will therefore be in favour of low wages, of low buying-power in the home market and of a price-level capable of being adjusted to meet the needs of the export trade. It will become an axiom of our economy that we live by our export trade. We shall be able to ask the reformers and the cranks how they propose to export if our goods exceed in price those of our competitors. 'What?' we shall say, 'you wish to fix prices! Do you realise that if, having done so, you happen to be faced by lower prices in some foreign country, you will be compelled either to change your price-level or to lose the whole of your export trade?' When we ask that question they will see, looming before them, the spectre of markets glutted with goods which cannot be sent abroad. For do not forget that, by that time, our industry will have been organised for foreign rather than for home trade and our agriculture will have been diverted into such channels as the breeding of pedigree stock and the production of milk.

"We shall be importing most of our food to pay the interest on loans made abroad. We cam alarm the politicians, if need be, by asking them how they propose to pay for people's food if they do not export more than they import. Believe me, my dear sir, those arguments and questions will effectually silence any kind of opposition to our wishes. Everybody, the Government, the Political Parties, the manufacturers, the merchants, even the farmers themselves, will be convinced of the absolute necessity of maintaining the export trade. They will be convinced therefore of the necessity of keeping our money stable with the monies of foreign countries, that is to say of maintaining a fixed foreign exchange by the use of gold as the international currency. They will all exert themselves to keep costs and wages as low as possible and thus to deprive the home market of the power to buy the home products. You will be assured, for ever, of a freely movable price-level."

Our banker shook his head.

"But, so far as I can see," he objected, "we shall not ourselves be allowed by you and the other International Bankers, to move that freely movable price-level."

"Oh, yes, you will. Indeed, we shall move it for you if you don't move it for yourselves. Our interests and your interests are the same. We are money-lenders, or rather lenders of promises to pay money. We need a plentiful supply of good, honest, hard working borrowers. The only way, as I have said, to secure such a supply is to induce men of the right type to embark upon industrial enterprises which require large amounts of capital for their initiation. How can we induce good borrowers to undertake such enterprises? You have already answered that question. By offering them the chance of a profit. In other words by making it clear that prices are going to rise. How can we make that clear? By giving loans to people, no matter where, who wish to build something, to make something.

"Let me give you an illustration. Business has slumped in this and other countries. Prices are low and labour, by reason of unemployment, is cheap. We, the International Bankers, have IOUs on our hands which we are anxious to lend. We know that the people of the Argentine are anxious to build a railway and are only waiting till they think prices have reached bottom in order to begin the work. We approach the Argentine government and offer it a loan. Our loan is accepted. As prices are very low in this country the order comes here. We begin to pay out money to steel works and other construction firms in this country. More labour is employed.

There is more buying-power, at once, in the home market. Prices, therefore, turn upward. It soon occurs to the local builder that there is likely to be an improved demand for small houses. He gets out plans and comes to you, the Home Bankers, with a proposition for a loan. And so on."

The International Banker rose and stood in front of the fire.

"And so," he said, "the boom begins. You get your IOUs working for you until a point is reached when prices and wages in this country have risen so high that it is no longer possible to export to foreign countries. Exports fall off, therefore, and fail to pay for imports. We, who are lending our IOUs to finance foreign trade become aware that, very soon, merchants will be asking us for gold to send abroad in payment for imported goods. We begin therefore to raise our rates of interest so as to stop borrowing. That is the signal to you to raise your rates also - for you know that if you go on lending at the old rates, in spite of our signal, exports will fall still further by reason of a further rise in home prices. We will be compelled in that case to part with still more gold and the outflow of gold will result in the withdrawal from yourselves of a corresponding quantity of notes of the National Bank which, under the system I am proposing, you will be allowed to count as equivalent to gold and on which, therefore, you will have lent ten times their value of IOUs.

"In other words disregard of our signal will inflict on you and on your clients the heavy penalty of a catastrophic fall in prices, which is likely, as you know, to cause a panic and lead to demands by your clients for real money far in excess of your holdings. Obviously you will wish to avoid that danger. You will therefore act at once on our signal and begin, gently at first, to raise your rates of interest to borrowers and to call in some of your loans.

As a result the fall in prices will be slow and gradual. You will profit by the higher rates of interest and you will be able to lend to us the IOUs you can no longer lend at home - for, with falling prices and costs, exporting will have begun again. This gradual rise and gradual fall of prices will not produce effects such as are produced by wild booms and violent slumps. There will be no panic when the fall takes place and consequently we shall not be plagued by Committees of Inquiry or by the attentions of currency cranks. The system will be semi-automatic. And there is another point... "

The International Banker held up his hand in a gesture which recalled that of a clergyman bestowing a blessing.

"There will be large numbers of people," he declared, "to whom this close linking together of all the nations of the world will make strong appeal on sentimental and humanitarian grounds. If we are attacked, we can reply that the foreign exchanges are the charter of internationalism. We can say that the world has become one in trade and commerce as it must, ultimately, become one in sympathy and in brotherhood. We can insist that the day has gone by when any nation, even the greatest, can live to itself. We can extol the blessings of a league of nations and speak with horror of nationalism and economic nationalism. We can proceed to discussions on disarmament. We shall, thus, rally to our support all the liberal elements of the community, all the humanitarian elements, all the pacifist elements, all the socialists. Our money will seem to be the cement of peoples, the enemy of war, the sure means to the world-state."

The International Banker's face expressed a lively satisfaction.

"Believe me," he concluded, "I mean what I say. Men are but animals, after all, greedy, hungry, selfish, of such nature that it is by their self-interest alone that you can hope to lead them. If we hold them in our debt, and make borrowers of them all, that is only the better to serve their highest and truest interests. Our power will be absolute, for there will be no escape from us. We shall use that power to unite the peoples, to reorganise industry and trade on a more remunerative basis and to combat everywhere the individualism which constitutes so serious a menace to human progress and human happiness."

VI REMEMBER THE MORATORIUM

The International Banker developed further his humanitarian views when he was called by the Government to advise them about the crisis and the way of preventing trouble in the future.

"The lesson," he said, "that I draw from the recent financial panic in this country is that we have been trying to grow rich at the expense of the rest of the world. We saw a chance of profit and seized it without regard to the needs of our neighbours. There was a wild orgy of spending, of borrowing; prices rose to fantastic heights and expectations of profit assumed grotesque proportions. Wages mounted up and a standard of living far above our means was indulged in. Now that the bubble has burst we are realising that no nation can afford to get out of touch, out of step, with its neighbours."

The Chief Minister nodded approval but the Home Minister displayed a less accommodating temper.

"If the banks had refused to lend so much money," he said, "the boom would not have attained such dimensions."

"I agree. The Home Bankers ought to have raised their rates of interest long before they did."

The Home Minister frowned.

"On the other hand lending stopped just when a great mass of goods was coming on to the market, that is to say, when more, and not less, money was needed."

"There had been gross over-production. The goods could not, by any means, have been sold at home. It was essential to bring about a fall in prices in order to get the goods into foreign markets and so save the producers from ruin."

"Suppose you had created more buying power for the home markets... "

"No, sir. Allow me, sir, to question your assertion that bankers create money. What we lend is our credit, the good name which honest dealing has built up and advertised. This credit is valuable only so long as we refrain from any action likely to shake it. It is valuable by reason of our knowledge of borrowers and their businesses, a knowledge difficult to acquire and costing much money in its acquisition. Why, sir, any man may set up as a banker. Any man may lend his credit. But there is credit and credit. Why does the public seek eagerly for one man's credit, give goods and service for it and take it in exchange for debt? Clearly because that credit is big with value. Why is another man's credit worthless? Because it has no value. Surely a man may sell the field he has tilled or the business he has created for what it is worth to his fellows?"

This speech won the approval of the Chief Minister who nodded gravely. But the Home Minister frowned once more.

"People borrow your IOUs," he said, "solely because they believe these promises can be converted into gold."

"No, sir. Everybody knows that a big run on a bank must break it."

"You are suggesting that what you lend is well worth the price asked for it." "Evidently, since people continue to pay the price we ask."

The Home Minister leaned across the table.

"Any roguery could be justified in that way," he declared. "In fact there is next to no gold behind your promises. We can therefore exclude that metal from our discussion. What are you lending, then? Your skill, you say; your good name; your business experience. But no borrower wants these things. What borrowers want is money - something with which they can buy things or pay wages."

"Quite so, we lend the means of buying and paying."

"It is the public which honours your promises by giving goods for them."

"You are saying that the public trusts, and so coverts, our promises. Would the public accept Mr X's promises? Of course not."

"Wait a moment. What the public is getting in

exchange for its goods are your promises to pay what you do not possess and never have possessed. Your skill and experience in the circumstances in which they are exercised are worth nothing to the public. Do you suggest that the banks which failed in the recent crisis had less skill and experience than you have? Everyone of you would have failed if we, the Government, had refused you the Moratorium. You told us that yourself. I say again that what you are lending is essentially worthless and has been proved to be worthless. But you are able to palm it off on the public because we, the Government, have, in fact, if not in name, given you the Nation's credit to play with."

The International Banker shrugged his shoulders. "How so?" he asked.

"The credit of any nation depends on its character and its resources. A nation without courage, without discipline, without skill or without honesty can possess no credit. Nobody could or would lend anything to such a nation."

"I agree cordially, my dear Home Minister."

"It follows, does it not, that what gives value to your promises-to-pay is the credit of the nations to whom these promises are issued?"

"What?"

"How much gold is there actually behind every £10 of your IOUs?"

The International Banker hesitated. The Home Minister made a quick gesture.

"Before the National Bank was allowed to issue notes to replace gold," the Home Minister said, "there was £1 in gold behind £10 of your IOUs. Today, since the new notes have appeared, there is considerably less. The National Bank will issue three £1 notes, roughly, for every £1 in gold it possesses. You will lend £10 of IOUs for every National Bank Note you possess. Consequently the gold backing behind your IOUs for £10 will be 6s 8d [about 33 pence - ed]. Do you agree?"

"Oh, yes."

"What would you say to a man who tried to pay a debt of £10 with six shillings and eight pence?"

"What has this got to do with banking?"

"Everything. The fact is that your IOUs are worth almost nothing." "They buy anything you like to buy with them."

"Exactly. Because the public thinks they possess real value."

"The public knows that we lend more promises to pay money than the actual amount of money in our hands."

"Not at all. What the public thinks is that you are lending good money, money earned by other people but entrusted to you for lending purposes. The idea that you are engaged in creating money out of nothing... "

"I deny that. We do not create money. What we do is to distribute goods." "How?"

"By lending our good name so that these goods may be disposed of."

"You mean by lending your promises to pay money, your IOUs?"

"These are our goods. You are at liberty, if you wish, to lend your good name in the same way. Our good name, it may be, would command a higher price than your good name."

This was spoken with a charming smile. But there was no answering smile on the Home Secretary's lips.

"What you are really saying," he exclaimed, "is that the public believes that you have money to lend, but does not believe that I am in that happy position."

"Well?"

"Whereas, in fact, you have no money to lend. You do not lend money at all. You lend only your promises to pay money and the moment any large number of persons asks for the fulfilment of these promises you come yelping to us for a Moratorium."

"Need we keep returning to that?"

"We must never for a moment depart from it. What

I am submitting is that you have accomplished a confidence trick by which you have convinced the public that you have money to lend."

"The public, as I have told you, knows exactly what we lend."

"I say that it knows nothing of the kind. Do you really suggest that the public is aware that your so-called deposits are in fact nothing but loans made by you?"

"How can I tell you that?"

"You will agree that it is the public which makes your IOUs valuable?" "It is always the consumer who makes goods valuable, is it not?" "Bogus goods?"

"Any goods. People soon cease to buy what they find to be bogus."

"Why, if that is so, do they go on buying your IOUs after you have all gone bankrupt? How can the promises-to-pay of a body of men who have had to be given a Moratorium, as the alternative to the repudiation of their debts, be worth anything the next morning?"

"The public is the judge of that, surely?"

"No, sir. The public is simply deceived. You have so bewildered and befogged the public mind that your statements are accepted as gospel. Thus you are able to lend people their own credit and charge them interest for so doing. The Moratorium was a gift to you from the Government. It allowed you to buy Government notes, that is to say Government IOUs with your IOUs. The Government, in other words, used the nation's credit to support your promises-to-pay. It actually allowed you to buy National Credit with your IOUs - for nothing, that is to say."

"But that was only one, conspicuous, example," the Home Minister continued, "of what is going on all the time inconspicuously. You are always, every day, engaged in seizing national credit for nothing.

That is what every coiner and utterer of false notes does. Money, remember, is a debt of the community to the holder of that money. When you create your IOUs you are putting the nation in your debt. You can go out with these IOUs and demand payment in goods and services - and get it too. During the Moratorium you bought National Notes, at other times you buy directly in the shops, or lend directly to borrowers - in both cases you are drawing on the national wealth by the mere process of signing your names. You are thus establishing claims to other people's goods without having earned these claims. Worse still, you are demanding interest on the unearned claims. Having secured the booty you are lending it out to its real owners."

The Home Minister's face was red. The International Banker flicked the ash from his cigar.

"I've heard this before," he declared in a tired voice.

"And will hear it again, I hope. The point I am

making is that the only backing money can have in this or any other country is goods and services, delivery of which must necessarily depend on the character and resources of the people - the national credit. When you tell me that my IOUs would not be borrowed or accepted in payment for anything, you are saying only that I am a less expert burglar of the national resources than yourself.

Your IOUs buy goods. Therefore they *are* money. You are consequently creating money no matter how you may try to cover up that fact by pretending that you are giving value... "

"Has our name no value?"

"Only in so far as you possess real goods or genuinely earned money. In any other circumstances, such value as people may choose to attach to your name is a false value, based on lack of knowledge. In other words the fact that people can be induced to buy or borrow bogus IOUs or bogus shares does not make these IOUs or these shares genuine."

Silence fell in the room. The Chief Minister moved uneasily in his chair. But the Home Minister remained full of fight.

"You admit, I take it," he demanded of the International Banker, "that what you call your 'deposits' are in fact loans to your customers?"

"A loan creates a deposit."

"Why do you call them 'deposits', then? The public understands by a 'deposit', money placed in a bank for safe keeping."

"We have our own technical expressions, you know."

"In fact every credit account in your ledgers is balanced by overdraft?" "That is one way of putting it."

"So that if you called up all the overdrafts all the credit accounts would necessarily disappear?? I mean over the system as a whole?"

"Possibly."

"One man's savings are another man's debts?" "Well?"

"And all the debts are, finally, debts to you. All the savings therefore exist solely at your good pleasure. You have only to stop lending and allow your debtors to pay you back in order to become possessed of the entire wealth of the country, all the savings and consequently all the claims to property of all kinds."

"We do not stop lending."

"Of course not. If you did that on any great scale people would find you out. Prices would fall to nothing and there would be Commissions of Inquiry." The Home Minister leaned forward.

"If we, the Government, choose to stabilise prices,"

he declared, "you will be compelled to go on lending on pain of having the lending done for you by the Government? Is that so?"

"We always go on lending."

"Then why object to a stabilization of prices?"

"Who told you that we object? On the contrary stability of the price-level is our chief concern. After all, we are the guardians of the nation's savings."

"The savings which are balanced by loans? The savings which are held in the form of your IOUs?"

"Why not?"

"Don't you see that the man who pays money into his bank thinks that it is real, genuine money which he is paying in? He has no idea that what he is paying in is merely a handful of your promises to pay money. Still less does he realize that this handful of promises was created by you in favour of somebody else who still owes it and who must, some day, pay it back.

How can that unknown debtor pay back his debt unless he first of all recovers it from its present owner or owners?"

The Home Minister's eyes flashed.

"In other words," he cried, "no matter what happens, these IOUs, which we have allowed to become nine-tenths of the money of this country, always belong to you. No matter who may acquire them temporarily you can always get them back again by refusing to lend and calling up your outstanding loans. Mr Smith may think he has £100 in the bank but he will soon find, when you are taking in sail, and calling up your loans, that his £100, like everybody else's money, has been furnished by you, its creators, with most serviceable wings. As your IOUs grow scarcer and scarcer prices will fall and as prices fall Mr Smith's business will cease to pay. He will then have to 'draw out' his little nest egg. Even if he is living on investments it will be the same. Dividends will fall. Taxes upon the incomes of those who have any money left will increase. So long as everybody uses your IOUs instead of money and so long as you continue to issue your IOUs only in the form of loans every soul in the land, rich or poor, creditor or debtor, must remain, forever, in your power. The fact that in a great community there are millions of debtors and creditors and that, in consequence, your activities are well hidden, does not alter the truth by a jot. You issue all the money in the country. You issue it all as loans, repayable with interest. Therefore you can, in theory at least, possess yourself of all the wealth in the country - the whole national credit. The claims against you, those 'hard earned savings' about which we hear so much, are balanced in every case by your claims against the community."

"My dear sir," the International Banker interrupted, "don't you see that you are giving away your own case? If our claims on the community are balanced by the community's claims on us, we can possess nothing at all."

"Do you give security for your loans?"

"Security? Why should we give security when we are the lenders?"

"I thought you told me a few days ago that every loan from a bank was an exchange of debts?"

"Quite. We take the house, or whatever the security may be; we owe that to its owner. He takes our credit, our promises-to-pay if you like. He owes that sum of money to us."

"Don't you see that what have been exchanged are promises - your promise to pay him; his promise to repay you. He gives security in the shape of his house. Why should not you give security also? Is your word so much better than his?" The Home Minister held up his hand as he spoke. He added, "Before you answer please remember the Moratorium."

"We are lending money. Money is its own security."

"Remember the Moratorium. And remember also that what you are lending are promises to pay money and not money itself."

There was no reply. The Home Minister bit his lip.

"In fact your promises are not backed by collateral security. (I mention the Moratorium once more.) Consequently the community's claims on you are worthless unless you choose to keep your promises to the community.

And we know from experience that you cannot do that in any time of crisis. You are a ship guaranteed not to sink in fine weather. Your debtors' promises, on the contrary, are anything but worthless, for they are supported by houses, land, cargoes, all the wealth of the nation. In other words the community has no enforcible claims on you whereas you have supplied yourselves with overwhelming claims on it. Any attempt by your creditors to enforce their so-called claims instantly reveals the fact that you are without substance. If your creditors become pressing they are punished by losing all their savings. You shut your doors and so acknowledge that your promises-to-pay are false promises - unless indeed the Government comes to your rescue with the Nation's credit."

"Do you suggest that we could call in all our loans?" the International Banker asked.

"In theory certainly. If you did you could not, of course, be paid in money. But you would be able, legally, to seize all the security left in your hands. My point is that your creditors, the people who have entrusted their savings to you, have no security - nothing but your promises. A broken promise has no market value, whereas a house can be lived in."

"We possess gold."

"Six shillings and eightpence worth against £10 of IOUs. Thirty IOUs for every golden pound. In the game of musical chairs only one person fails to secure a seat; in your game the number of the dispossessed, supposing each has a claim for one golden pound and all present their claims on the same day, with be twenty nine. Talk about lotteries! Let me tell you, therefore, that the Government is now thinking about a scheme to stabilize the price-level so that for the future there will be neither booms nor slumps, neither sharp rises nor severe falls."

The Home Minister's voice carried a note of triumph, which proclaimed the fact that it was he who had persuaded his colleagues in the Cabinet to agree to the reform. But the International Banker was no longer looking at the Home Minister. He had turned to the Chief Minister.

"Is this true?" he asked, "That you propose to fix prices?"

"We had some idea of doing something of the sort. I think, though, that you had better ask the Treasurer. As a matter of fact, I have no expert knowledge about finance."

"Evidently not."

"The Treasurer," the Home Secretary interpolated, "has consented to try stabilizing prices."

"Really?"

The International Banker no longer looked like a man who had come to argue. He looked like the President of a Court Martial making ready to promulgate sentence. He addressed himself once more to the Chief Minister.

"Surely," he asked, "you know something about finance now - after all that we have just heard?"

His tones were polite but crisp. The Chief Minister flapped his hands.

"Believe me, no. My brain is political, not financial. These are questions of currency and credit. It often seems to me that anybody may be right. Mind you, though, I still think it would be a good thing if we could fix prices - or at any rate steady them a bit - for the sake of the whole country."

The International Banker drew near.

"You have considered the effect of your proposal, I take it, on our export trade?" he demanded.

"Oh, we had no idea of trying to fix the price of exports." "How can you fix prices without fixing the price of exports?" The Chief Minister turned to the Home Minister.

"You said there was some way of doing that, didn't you?" he asked.

"I said we ought to leave exports to take care of themselves. If we don't export enough to pay for our imports the value of our money, as compared with foreign monies, will fall; that will prevent us from buying so much abroad and so restore the balance between exports and imports."

"There's just one little snag in that pretty picture,"

the International Banker told the Chief Minister.

"Well?"

"Prices at home will rise."

The Chief Minister looked anxious. "Why so?" he asked.

"Because imports will have been cut down and exports increased. There will be less goods in the markets at home."

"Then we shall produce more goods."

"At higher prices, seeing that you must buy your raw materials abroad." The Home Minister shook his head.

"We are exporting much more than we import at the present moment," he declared.

"Quite so, because your money is sound. Because your money can look other people's money in the face and you are able, therefore, to buy food and raw materials at world prices. A country with a debased money cannot do these things. The very best it can hope to do is to supply its own domestic needs."

"Which is the important thing. What does it matter how much we export if our people are happy and prosperous?"

"You will have to accept a lower standard of living."

"Why?"

"Why? Because you will be getting less for your debased money." The Home Minister bit his lip.

"Look here, sir, if I wanted to argue as if a nation lived only to ship its wealth out of the country to foreigners, I would say that our debased money, as you call it, ought to help us to export. If 10s (50 pence - ed) in foreign money is worth £1 here then obviously we can afford to sell cheaper than foreigners. But I don't want to argue on these lines at all because I do not believe that a nation exists solely to make goods for foreign markets. What I want to see is a home market capable of buying home products. We shall have a surplus of certain goods and that superabundance we can properly exchange for the foreign goods we want. I know that such a system means getting out of step, as you call it, with the rest of the world. It means making and buying as many of our own goods as we can make and as we can use at home. It means a big home market, the industrialists buying from the farmers and the farmers buying from the industrialists. It means the restoration of agriculture to the position of the most important of our industries... "

"Agriculture is still our biggest industry."

"I was not thinking about bigness. I was thinking about the association of men with their native soil, about the life of villages, about the breed to which we belong. I have no hostility to the towns, but towns without a setting of tilled fields are trees without roots."

The International Banker turned again towards the Chief Minister. "Are these your views, sir?" he asked.

"I'm not sure. I dislike the idea of living to ourselves, within narrow limits. The world, it seems to me, must be treated as a single unit."

"I agree with you."

"After all," the Chief Minister went on, "we are a commonwealth. The tribes have been merged in the kingdoms; the kingdoms have disappeared within the frontiers of empires. We think now in terms of races and peoples. We are beginning to think in terms of the human race, the universal people. All are partners in our world-state, our great commonwealth. It is for the good of all men that the statesmen of the future must work."

"A mutual benefit society."

"Precisely. One law, one peace, one inheritance."

"Only finance," the International Banker said, "can give the world these blessings. Money is the guarantor of a just and free distribution of wealth." The International Banker approached nearer to the Chief Minister. "If the world were one," he said, "we should grow wheat where wheat may most easily and cheaply be grown. We should grow cotton where the climate and the soil invite to the cultivation of that crop. Where the coal fields lie, there we should place our heavy industries. And so on. Surely there would be benefit for all in this arrangement, this co-operation? It would break down the walls of nationalism, of Parochialism, of racial jealousies and class antagonism. We should recognise our brotherhood. We should respect each other's rights as men, the children and offspring of the same earth-mother. What a vision! The whole earth developed and cultivated in the best possible way for the benefit of each one of us. Each of us a partner, a shareholder in the World Ltd. [now it would be termed the World PLC - ed], concerned only to see that each of us receives his or her share. How can nationalism be mentioned in the same breath with this vision?

What is Nationalism? A narrow, greedy living for self. Disregard of the interests of others. Contempt of foreigners. Hostility to the people of the next parish, even. Men, I think, ought to pray to be delivered from such a fate. If Finance really deserved all the Home Minister has spoken against it and yet was able to defeat the nationalist spirit in the gate, Finance would remain the greatest benefactor of us all."

He had flushed with the wine of his oratory. The Chief Minister's cheeks, too, were glowing. His eyes were bright.

"I'm bound to say," he cried, "that I agree with you. I have spent my whole life contending against the spirit of Nationalism and its horrible accompaniment of War. It seems to me that anything which breaks down the barriers between peoples must be for humanity's benefit.

Internationalism means disarmament, it means intercourse between men, it means world-friendship."

The Chief Minister spoke with an ease which made sharp contrast with his diffidence in discussing finance. He was back again in his element. He breathed freely.

"The truth, of course, is," the Home Minister said, "that it is financial internationalism which breeds war. Look at the facts. International Bankers lend their IOUs in such a way that gold is not, normally, asked for. In other words the borrowers are not normally in the position of wishing to convert the promises to pay money into money itself - into gold. But if the balance of trade gets badly upset, if outgoings greatly exceed incomings or incomings outgoings, then a condition of affairs arise in which gold is likely to be asked for.

"In the case where a country is not exporting enough to pay for its imports, gold will be shipped abroad to pay for the difference and square the bill - for if that is not done the money of the country with a deficiency of exports must fall in value relatively to the money of the country with which it is in a business relationship.

"In other words the Exchange will move against the country with a deficiency of exports because more people will be using its money to buy foreign money than will be using foreign money to buy its money. The export of gold prevents this fall in the Exchange. But, since International Bankers, like Home Bankers, are lending promises to pay ten times the quantity of money which they actually possess, it is obvious that strict limits are set to the export of gold. If the 'drain of gold', as it is called, goes on for any considerable length of time all the International Bankers will be compelled to close their doors.

"In fact, as we have just seen," the Home Minister continued, "the International Bankers protect themselves by refusing to lend and trying to call up as many as possible of their existing loans - just as, in similar circumstances, the Home Bankers do. The result is that foreign trade stops and huge masses of goods designed for export are thrown on the home market. Prices crash and panic occurs. The Home Market, therefore, lives in great fear of a falling off of exports and is even anxious that this should be prevented by some device which will have the effect of preventing a rise of prices at home. The Home Market, in fact, is ready to submit its buying power to the good pleasure of International Bankers... "

"How little you understand this matter," the International Banker exclaimed. "What we propose is not a dictatorship over the price-level here at home, but a co-ordination of that level with the world price-level."

"Of course. So that nowhere on earth may anyone pay you less for your IOUs that the largest rate of interest anyone on earth is willing to pay. If a country is paying high wages and so becoming possessed of buying power in the home market... "

"Why do you always speak as if wages and buying power were the same thing?"

"Because they are the same thing. It is the wages paid out to the work people which buy the products of industry. If big wages are paid the home market has a big buying power and can absorb large quantities of goods. When wages are reduced many of these goods cannot any longer be sold at home and must therefore be hurried into foreign markets. Low wages in other words mean beg exports and so a 'favourable' balance of trade - as you call an excess of exports over imports. Consequently when wages begin to rise International Finance begins to act. It takes money out of the home market and so makes both the existing level of prices and the existing level of wages impossible. Long before there is any substantial loss of export trade - at the very whisper of rising wages - all the devices so well known to you and your colleagues are brought into operation. You clamour to have the Bank Rate raised, so that producers at home may be discouraged from further borrowing. The effect is a fall of prices and a sudden flow of goods towards the ports. What with your own IOUs and the IOUs of the Home Bankers, who can no longer find borrowers at their doors, you are ready to finance any quantity of exports.

"In other words you have snatched away buying power from the home market to give that buying power to foreign markets. The home workers lose part of, or the whole of, their wages; what they lose comes at once to you to be lent by you outside of the country. I spoke a short time ago about the danger to you of fixed prices. In fact fixed prices imply fixed costs, that is to say fixed wages. The truth is that stabilization of the foreign exchanges - of the value of money - must necessarily be threatened by any attempt to stabilize wages - even by so small an attempt as the payment of 'doles'. If, under your system, wages in one country are reduced wages in all other countries ***must be reduced*** *also*. For if any country does not, in such circumstances, reduce its wages it will fail to export. If it fails to export you, the International Bankers operating in that country, will be asked to make good your promises to pay. You will be asked for gold. You will resist that demand by bringing foreign trade to an end in the way we have been discussing. If these measures, which are bound to bring about a fall of prices, fail to bring about a fall of wages also, then you will have to ask for a Moratorium - in other words the country with the high wages will be compelled to come off the gold standard. For you possess little gold and many people will have claims for gold against you and through you against the National Bank. The gold standard is a method of keeping money in any one country pegged to the monies of all other countries. It is the most efficient peg for this purpose which has ever been found. When prices are fixed, or when wages are fixed, the gold standard must break down sooner or later... "

The Chief Minister made an impatient gesture.

"What has that to do with international co-operation?" he asked.

"Everything. The people whom International Finance is playing off against each other are not merely the merchants and industrialists of the world. The wage-earners in every country are being pitted against the wage-earners in every other country. The attack on wages is everlasting and it is conducted by means of the wage-earners themselves who have nothing to hope for unless they can produce cheaply, that is to say unless they will accept lower wages than all their competitors.

'Tighten your belts, my boys, and we shall take their trade away from them,' is, necessarily, the cry of every industrial leader. What else can he say? If his men refuse to 'fight' - and the parallel with a battle is a close one - he will soon be out of business himself. In such circumstances a country with highly organized Trade Unions or with a satisfactory scale of unemployment-pay is bound to be left behind while the gold standard remains in operation. Its people will not cease to feel the foreign knife at their throats. Hatred and fear will make real soldiers of such people."

The Home Minister raised his arm and pointed at the International Banker.

"What are you doing just now?" he demanded. "Everywhere I hear nothing but demands for lower wages so that we may 'regain' our position as an exporting nation. There are strikes and lockouts. The men, naturally, blame their masters; the masters blame their men. Both are helpless in your hands, since it is you who control the quantity of money in their markets. As things stand half the population will soon be unemployed unless wages are cut. If wages are not cut half the businesses will be bankrupt. And when wages have been cut the whole hideous cycle will begin once more. Do you wonder that, in such circumstances, Communism and Socialism, both of them will-o'-the-wisps, flourish? Do you wonder that class is set against class? Master against man? Nation against nation? Nobody suspects the true enemy. Nobody sees that your worthless IOUs are the real cause of his troubles or that, if what you were lending was honest money, there would be neither need nor wish for this fixing of

Exchanges and for all the frantic efforts you make to prevent a demand for gold on the part of those to whom you have lent promises to pay that metal. You are breaking up the structure not of homes only but of nations. You are setting nation against nation and people against people. Your internationalism is another name for a dreadful scramble for food and shelter by all the races of mankind against all the races of mankind. It is, as I sincerely believe, the most evil system ever devised."

VII   INTERNATIONAL FINANCE

A few days later the public was informed that the Home Minister had resigned his office. The following letters were published:

From the Home Minister to the Chief Minister.

"My dear Chief Minister,

"I think you will agree that our inability to take the same view about the measures necessary for dealing with the present crisis makes it essential that I should place my resignation in your hands. As you know, I am in favour of nationalization of credit and the use of some system of price control. This would entail the abandonment of any attempt to stabilize the foreign exchange. You, for your part, look to stabilization of the exchanges to afford those happier conditions of life which both of us are so anxious to secure.

"I am, etc."

From the Chief Minister to the Home Minister.

"My dear Colleague,

"While I regret your decision, I cannot say that I am surprised by it. For, as you justly observe, the methods that you favour are incompatible with those which, in common with all my present colleagues, I feel to be necessary in our difficult and anxious circumstances. A fixed and stabilized exchange offers to our merchants and traders the indispensable foundation of business. It secures the food of the People. It guarantees the supply of those raw materials without which our industry must come to a standstill.

"Advantages so great, it seems to me, ought not to be sacrificed to such hopes as may be entertained that an attempt to control prices would raise the standard of living of our people. A standard of living which cannot be maintained is little better, I fear, than a piece of political window-dressing. It is likely to inflict cruel disappointment; it cannot afford a true basis of progress.

"Moreover, since no nation today can hope to live to itself, any policy which tends towards isolation stands, it seems to me, self-condemned. We must march with humanity towards the unification of the world.

"I am, etc."

The Chief Minister's letter had an excellent reception in the Press.

"His fellow countrymen," said one important newspaper, "have reason to be grateful to him for his clear understanding of the issues involved. This is not solely a financial question. The recent crisis cannot be ascribed wholly to monetary causes. The truth is that a system the success of which depends on its elasticity has grown rigid.. If lenders were rash, borrowers were not less so. Those producers who expected the community to guarantee in perpetuity what was in fact a speculative bubble, an orgy of inflation, displayed not only ignorance about the bases of sound finance but also an astonishing disregard of the necessities of foreign trade. It is proper, therefore, to repeat, as the Chief Minister repeats, that a stable exchange guarantees the food of the People and the supply of raw materials. There is no advantage of class or section which ought, for a moment, to be preferred to this national advantage. How, if we do not export, can we pay for our imports? An inflated standard of living, in face of rising food prices, is just as impossible today as it has ever been in the past.

"Honest and patriotic men, therefore, will rejoice that the leadership of the nation rests in the hands of a statesman possessed of real courage. The acid test of democracy, after all, is its readiness to face unpleasant truths and to take such action as will supply the remedy for situations which have become impossible. We have lived beyond our means; we must make ready, at once, to live within them. We have allowed ourselves to spend what, in fact, we had not earned; we must economise; we must tighten our belts. If wages are unjustifiably high they must fall. If costs are too great to enable us to compete successfully in foreign markets, costs must be reduced."

Another newspaper, of a more commercial complexion, deplored the levity of the Home Minister's suggestions.

"Does he fail to understand," this journal asked,

"that the interest which we receive from foreign investments and from the financing of foreign trade helps to pay for the food supply of our People? Happily for our beloved country the Chief Minister sees that attempts to buy abroad with unsound money are foredoomed to failure. In declaring, as in effect he has done, for a speedy return to the gold standard and to the principles of sound finance, he has declared for honesty and for the sanctity of contracts, and City men, at any rate, will thank him.

"For it cannot be too widely that the obligation to give gold in exchange for credit instruments, that is to say to honour one's promise to pay gold upon demand, is the indispensable safeguard of all monetary contracts. It is because he knows that his clients are entitled to ask him to make good in gold the promises which he has offered them, that a banker is forced, at all times, to keep his position liquid and so to avoid speculation. This applies to International as well as to Home Bankers. The moment gold begins to leave the country we have positive proof that our exports are falling below the limits of safety. From that moment investment in the home market is speculation, because it constitutes a refusal to face the fact that we are consuming more than we produce."

The former Home Minister ventured to reply to this last newspaper.

"It boils down to this," he wrote, "that since our markets are glutted with goods we must tighten our belts and economise. And if we consume what we have produced we are living beyond our means. It is perfectly true, as you say, that the gold standard prevents our money from losing value in terms of foreign currencies. But this is only another way of saying that the gold standard prevents wages in this country from rising above wages anywhere else or from remaining high when wages anywhere else have fallen. We are not allowed to consume more of out goods than the lowest paid workers in the world are consuming of their goods. Consequently we must export what may not be consumed. If foreign markets cannot absorb the mass of products pouring into them then further cuts in prices and wages will be necessary - or failing that the destruction of the products till a point is reached at which scarcity will begin to make its influence felt.

"From every point of view, except that of money-lending, the system is crazy. It would be crazy, even from the money-lender's standpoint if money-lending was, in fact, taking place. For a man who had lent money, and not merely promises to pay it, would have nothing to fear from an expansion of production. The root of our troubles is *the lending of IOUs by men who do not possess the money necessary to make good these promises to pay.* Our bankers, whether home or international, are all in the same position. All have lent promises to pay ten times the quantity of legal tender money in their possession. All are terrified that demands may be made upon them for the redemption of their promises in such quantity as to exhaust their small holdings of actual money, and so bring them to ruin.

The gold standard and all the other devices for keeping the Foreign Exchanges fixed and stable are, in fact, safeguards against 'runs' on banks which, all the time, are in a condition of insolvency. So long as exports, whether 'visible' or 'invisible' balance and pay for imports there will be no demands for actual money. This is the true explanation of the passionate interest which the export trade arouses and this is the real reason why it is asserted that a country which is surrendering its goods in exchange, often, for nothing more substantial than paper receipts, is richer and in better case than a country which is consuming its goods. That the system is enormously profitable to the world's usurers is, of course, true. But they are a handful of men; the mass of mankind is being sold into slavery.

"I fully admit that a country cannot without resort to dumping possess a 'favourable' balance of trade and a wage level higher than that of its neighbours. If we are to export more than we import we must hold our wages down and keep them down. Rigid exchanges and rigid wages are impossible side by side. Of the two I prefer the rigid wages, or rather wages high enough to buy all our products except the super-abundance which we cannot consume because we do not want it. This super-abundance is ample, as things now stand, to pay for all the food and raw materials that we require.

"It is obvious, however, that there is no place for the existing financial system inside the scheme I am advocating. For, under my scheme, exports would be left to take care of themselves and exchanges would be allowed to fluctuate freely. The emptying of the home market of buying power would not be tolerated. In such circumstances the best of the producers would soon get out of debt and cease to need to borrow; and usury, in consequence, would fall on evil days. The existing system, indeed, has only two objects - namely, to secure to usury a continuous supply of credit-worthy borrowers and to make it possible for usurers to lend promises to pay (IOUs) far in excess of their actual holdings of money. These two objects, being served, make our bankers our masters and place them in unchallenged control, and even ownership, of the whole of the real wealth of the world. You may call this by any name you choose - Internationalism or World Trade or human co-operation. Its real character is slavery.

"Finance has conquered the universe quite as effectually as the hordes of Ghengis Khan or of Timur the Lame conquered the nations which opposed them. Not only so, we have developed and are developing the slave-mind. We glory in our shame and extol the gods of our enemies. Religion, morality, even the processes of thought, are changing. The great, basal lie that a society may be founded on false promises is permeating all minds with the corruption of magic. Our god dwells not in the Heavens but in the counting house, where, with a pen in his hand, any clerk can perform the miracle of trans-substantiation which changes ink into land and houses and food."

VIII THE GOLD STANDARD

The Home Minister's letter brought a reply from a Bishop which was published a few days later.

"It must," the Bishop wrote, "be a matter of regret to many Christian people that the former Home Minister should have chosen to mingle religion with his politics. He has accused us all, and notably perhaps, by implication, the Churches, of having surrendered both faith and morality in obedience to those whom he calls our financial masters. An accusation so sweeping and so violent must always be difficult to refute but it may be allowed to one who has no expert knowledge of finance and but little knowledge of politics, to say that a cause is scarcely likely to be advanced in public regard by methods which, in effect, cast a doubt upon the sincerity of all who oppose it. Is our Chief Minister, are his colleagues, then, mere dupes of the financial interest? Is the Parliament of the Nation, likewise, a dupe? Does the whole body of public opinion in this, and all other lands, incline fatuously towards what is, according to the former Home Minister, at best a swindle and at worst a crime against God and man?

"It is only necessary, as I believe, to state the question in this way in order to reach a sound conclusion. It is easy for the former Home Minister to write that the foreign exchanges ought to be allowed to take care of themselves; but that means that those among our people who may have invested their savings abroad are to receive a premium over those who, on grounds possibly of conscience, have chosen to invest at home. If I buy French rentes when £1 is worth 100 francs and sell them when 50 francs are able to purchase £1, I have doubled my capital. But my gain is being paid for surely by those of my fellow countrymen who are compelled to buy French goods. A fixed exchange, as it seems to me, guarantees that justice shall be done as between buyer and seller, the owner of investments and the purchaser of goods.

"It has now, as I understand, been agreed that when gold leaves this country a corresponding amount of money in the form of notes shall be removed from circulation. This is likely to cause a fall of prices and so of wages. But the wage-earner ought to remember that his present sacrifice will be made good to him in cheaper foodstuffs. The value of a wage, after all, consists in its buying-power. To suggest therefore that a fall in the wage-level means a fall in the standard of living is both unfair and untrue. It need mean nothing of the sort.

"We enjoy today, in this our beloved land, the inestimable blessings of an ordered liberty. The fact that the former Home Minister is able to write as he has done about those that he calls 'conquerors' and 'tyrants' seems to me to disprove his accusations. Do conquerors and tyrants permit criticism of their actions? Our Press is free; we are entitled to express our opinions openly, and freely; we can come and go as we choose. Have 'slaves' ever, anywhere, enjoyed such advantages? I say, without hesitation or fear of contradiction, that this land of ours is governed according to Christian principles. Our people are immeasurably better off than any other people have ever been at any earlier time. In sobriety and peace they are leading lives which, from year to year, are being enriched by the good gifts of science and of education. A Christian, even in days of anxiety, cannot but rejoice at these manifestations of Providence. *Sursum Corda.* It is so fatally easy to criticise; but the critic, as a very wise man has reminded us, reveals himself."

The Home Minister, on reading this letter, went to the Bishop's palace. He laid a copy of the paper containing the Bishop's letter on the Bishop's desk.

"I've come to answer you," he declared, "as man to man. These letters to the newspapers are futile."

The Bishop looked startled. But he extended a welcoming hand.

"By all means," he said in tones that were not free from anxiety. "This question of a fixed exchange? You say it guarantees justice as between buyer and seller, the owner of investments and the purchaser of goods."

The Home Minister paused. An inclination of the Bishop's white head answered him.

"That is exactly, believe me, what a fixed exchange does not guarantee. Let us take buyer and seller first. If the exchange is fixed and the price-level allowed to fluctuate their contracts with one another may be changed in the sense that one or other may obtain an uncovenanted benefit. If I buy an article at £1 and, before the article can be delivered to me, the cost of producing it has fallen to 10s, the seller will get the advantage.

Had the cost risen to 30s instead of falling, the advantage would have come to me. This is, more or less, exactly what happens when the exchange is allowed to fluctuate and prices are fixed. In other words buyers and sellers suffer under either system. If it is not the exchange that they have to watch it is the price-level; and if it is not the price-level it is the exchange. This applies to investors in foreign businesses who buy ordinary shares in these businesses. But it does not apply when exchanges are fixed to the holders of *rentes* and other Government bonds."

The Home Minister leaned forward.

"What is the difference between an ordinary share in a business and a debenture?" he asked.

"The debenture is safer than the ordinary share, isn't it?" "Why is it safer?"

The Bishop shook his head.

"I'm afraid," he said, "that I am not well up in these matters."

"I'll tell you. Because a debenture is not a share at all. The shareholder in a company is a partner in the business. He takes risks. If the company earns no profits he gets no dividend; if the company goes bankrupt he loses his whole investment. Compare this with the position of the debenture holder. A debenture holder has no share in the business. He has merely lent money to the business. If the company loses, he does not share in the loss. If the company goes bankrupt, he seizes its lands, its buildings, all it has. In other words a debenture holder is a money-lender. He takes security for his loans just as a banker does. In consequence what he is interested in is not the price-level but the value of money. He wants goods to be cheap so that his money may buy more and more of them. He wants his money to be dear.

"There are many kinds of debentures. By far the most important kind are loans made to Governments on the security of the national income. These gilt-edged securities, as they are called, carry a fixed rate of interest. If Governments are poor, weak, desperate, they are still under the necessity of paying the same sums of money to their bondholders as in more prosperous days. And these bondholders will, if they can, wring out of those Governments the very last drop of blood.

"It is obvious, therefore, that bondholders, debenture holders, and also mortgage-holders stand in an entirely different category from ordinary shareholders. They are moneylenders whereas shareholders are merchants. Merchants, as we have seen, have nothing to lose from a free exchange. Changes as between the values of, say, French and German money or English and French money, need not trouble them more than changes as between the values of money and goods. If you give them a guarantee that the £1 will maintain a more or less constant buying power in the home market, they can make allowances for ups and downs as between the home markets and foreign markets. Under a fixed foreign exchange they have to watch price movements; under a controlled price level they will have to watch foreign exchange movements. It is six of one and half a dozen of the other.

But the position of the holders of debts (government debts, debentures, mortgages) is different. If the exchange is fixed these people can invest where they choose and rest assured that when they bring their money home again it will have lost nothing of its value."

"And gained nothing... "

"Quite. It works both ways, of course. The point I am coming to is that the bankers of the world are money-lenders and not merchants. They lend their promises-to-pay not as partners, but as creditors. The securities which they hold against their IOUs are, generally speaking, Government bonds, debentures or mortgages."

The Bishop held up his hand.

"But surely, my dear sir," he exclaimed, "that is only reasonable? A banker, as the trustee of other men's savings, cannot take risks."

"Bankers take such risks all the time as is not dreamed of by one in a million of their clients. What you have mentioned is, of course, the official explanation of the banker's preference for debts as opposed to partnerships. But there is another explanation which nobody ever hears about. These bonds and debentures and mortgages have one supreme merit in the eyes of money-lenders. They have to be repaid in full and they carry a fixed rate of interest. In other words they are, more or less, independent of the price level. If prices fall, shareholders may be ruined; but bondholders will be better off than before because their money will buy more. They will go on gaining until a point is reached at which payment of interest by borrowers can no longer be made. At that point the bondholders are able to seize the lands or buildings which have been pledged to them. In the case of Governments they are able to demand increased taxation and diminished expenditure on public services and works."

"A debt is a debt, you know."

"Quite. I am not denying that. If a debt has been incurred it ought, certainly, to be repaid. That is not what I am driving at. What I am concerned to show you is that the bondholders, the financial system, is in a position, when and if it chooses, to ruin its debtors and seize their property. Let me give you an example. I am a banker. I lend John Smith £1,000 on the security of his factory and the land on which it is standing. Next I call up some of my other loans and so diminish buying power inn the area in which John Smith conducts his business. In consequence of this shrinkage of buying power, or 'demand', prices fall and John Smith can no longer earn a profit. As he must pay me the interest on my loan, he now proceeds to cut down his staff of employees and to install labour-saving machinery. But I continue, day after day, to call up loans and to refuse to make new loans. Prices go on falling and, at last, John Smith comes to the end of his resources. He cannot reduce his staff any further without closing down. And he cannot afford to close down. He has to intimate to me that he will be unable to meet the interest on his debentures.

"I now seize his business and put it up for sale. The best bid is £800. So I take the business myself as payment for my loan. A little later I begin to lend again and prices begin to rise. John Smith's factory and plant are now worth having because there is a growing demand for the kind of goods he used to make. So I sell the business for £5,000 and put £4,200 in my own pocket. Do you follow?"

The Bishop's face wore a new, anxious expression.

"It cannot be as bad as that," he exclaimed in a whisper.

"It's quite as bad as that. But my example does not present the whole picture. An important element has been omitted. I have spoken as if the banker, in such a deal, was a free agent. He is not."

"Oh!"

"The free agent is not the Home Banker but the International Banker. It is when the International Banker finds that he can get higher rates of interest in some foreign country that the procession of disasters which I have described begins. For, unless exports increase to keep pace with the outflow of IOUs... "

"Forgive me, I don't follow you."

"When a loan of money is made abroad that is equivalent to an increase of imports into the country from which the loan has been made."

"Why?"

"A loan does not pay for imports."

The Bishop shook his head.

"I never could understand these extremely complicated ideas," he declared hopelessly.

"It isn't difficult if you remember that under the present system every country tries to balance, and so pay for, its imports with its exports and thus to avoid sending money, in the form of gold, abroad. The point about a loan made to foreigners is that it upsets the balance of trade. If the loan goes out in the form of goods all will be well; but if it goes out in the form of gold... "

"It can't go out in the form of goods unless the foreigners want the goods."

"Quite so. But the foreigners would not borrow unless they wanted goods. The real question is: are our goods as cheap as other people's goods? If not, the foreigner who has asked for the loan will take gold and use it to buy goods elsewhere. In that case exactly the same position will have arisen as arises when exports do not balance and so pay for imports. The bankers making the foreign loan will be asked to pay, not IOUs, but money, gold. As they possess only one-tenth of the money they have promised to pay they cannot, of course, meet such a demand. In fact, however, the mere threat that gold may be asked for is enough to bring prices down - for at this threat all lenders at once begin to shorten sail.

Consequently the loan to the foreigners which was made because better terms were offered abroad than were being offered at home, has, as its first effect, enforced a fall of prices in the home market and so of course - a fall of wages. Exports are thus increased and the loan goes abroad not in the form of gold but in the form of goods; the loan, in other words, acts like an import. It has to be 'met' by exports. Hence the name 'invisible import', which is usually applied to it. There is no import in actual fact; on the contrary, there is danger of an export of gold. That danger is avoided by so far reducing wages that a larger volume of exports of goods can be sent out of the country."

The Home Minister paused for a moment.

"I do hope I am making myself clear," he went on. "The mere fact that gold leaves a country matters nothing to anybody since nobody eats the metal. But it matters tremendously to a man who is lending promises to pay ten times the quantity of gold which he possesses. The real anxiety about an export of gold is not the fact of export but the fact that the gold has been asked for. Not one of the International Bankers can stand such a demand for any length of time because not one of them holds more than a tenth part of the money he has promised to pay.

"In other words the whole trouble resides in the private creation of IOUs to serve as money. The banker is trying to convince the world that a lie - namely, that he can fulfil his promises to pay ten times as much money as he possesses, is true. The only way in which he can make the lie look like truth is to prevent the holders of his IOUs from asking for their money. Our present banking system is therefore designed primarily to prevent demands being made for real money whether inside of the country or outside of it, whether in the form of notes of the national bank or of gold.

Bankers keep urging their clients to use more cheques, that is IOUs, and by implication less money. No bank can stand a 'run' which means that no bank can make good more than a very small proportion of its promises.

"At the same time every banker wants to get as much for these false promises of his as the world will give him. He wants therefore to be able to change his IOUs from one kind of money into another kind of money at a moment's notice. If, for example, I have lent IOUs for £1,000 in England and find that there is a borrower in France who will pay me a higher rate of interest than my English borrower, I want to be able to call up my loan and change it, instantly, into IOUs for, say, 100,000 francs. But I don't want to be asked to honour my IOUs in the process by giving gold for

them. I want the movement of goods to follow my loans in such a way that, no matter what I may do exports everywhere will pay for imports and no demands will therefore be made upon me for gold."

"Please explain to me," the Bishop interrupted, "how these demands for gold arise. If I make a loan to France don't I pay that loan in pounds?"

"No. If the worst comes to the worst you buy francs with pounds. You part with your pounds for gold and use the gold to buy francs."

"The worst comes to the worst?"

"I mean if the French don't use their loan to buy goods in England." "What happens if they do buy goods in England?"

"Then you pay the makers of the goods. You pay them by means of cheques drawn on yourself; by means, in other words, of promises-to-pay, of IOUs. That, of course, costs you nothing."

"What!"

"My dear Bishop, the whole object of international usury is to compel governments and peoples to compete with one another for the IOUs of the financiers. People will not compete for loans unless they need them. How can people be made to need loans? In what circumstances does a man or a company usually borrow? Surely when that man or that company lacks money either to carry on or to develop his business. Men with ample capital of their own do not borrow. Very well then, it is the aim of the financial system to prevent good borrowers from accumulating money of their own. That may be said to be the financial system's first and most important aim. Ask yourself in what circumstances men tend to accumulate capital. 'Is it not when prices are rising or when, having risen, prices are remaining more or less stable?' This is the position of affairs during an ordinary period of prosperity in trade. Obviously the financial system cannot allow such a state of affairs to continue indefinitely. What would happen if such a state of affairs did continue would be that many credit-worthy borrowers would become too rich to want to borrow at all and that, in consequence, loans would have to be made to less and less desirable recipients.

"The financial system protects those who live by it against this danger. As prices rise, more and more actual money is needed in shops and markets. Bankers are compelled, to a greater and greater extent, to honour their promises to pay. Their customers present cheques and ask for cash. Their stores of real money become depleted and they begin, in consequence, to stop lending and to call in loans so that they may not be caught out by a 'run'. When they stop lending prices of course fall and the men with money soon lose it and become good borrowers once more.

"High prices at home, therefore, threaten the Home Bankers by forcing them to part with real money. And that threat is soon passed on to the International

Bankers because high-priced goods cannot be sold abroad. Exports fall and no longer pay for imports and International Bankers, in their turn, are asked to make good their promises in money - in gold. Both Home and International Bankers therefore must, on pain of catastrophe, bring any rise of prices to an end or (it amounts to the same thing) compel a fall of prices if somebody else in the world is producing more cheaply.

"In a sense the system works automatically. If prices are too high in any country, that country will not be able to export. Goods will therefore pile up at home and prices will break. But we must be careful not to be led away by this aspect of the matter for it is obvious that, if the foreign exchange was free to move, high prices at home would not constitute an obstacle to the export trade. Our money would lose value the moment our exports did not pay for our imports. This fall in the value of our money would enable us to sell still in foreign markets because what cost £1 at home would be selling for, say, 15s. [75 pence - ed] abroad. (Owing to the fact that our £1 was worth now, in other countries, only 15s.)"

The Bishop shook his head.

"Surely that would suit the bankers better than the present system?" he said. "If the exchanges were allowed to fluctuate, they could not be asked to pay gold for their IOUs."

"No. But then their control of the price level would be gone. The moment it was discovered that a fluctuating exchange *unpegged in any way*, is harmless to trade, price-levels would be maintained by public agitation against anything which moneylenders might say. Would businessmen, who knew that they had nothing to fear, even as exporters, from a home market which was possessed of a high degree of buying power, allow their home market to be emptied of that buying power? Of course not. On the contrary it would soon be insisted that, as more goods were produced, more money should be issued to ensure their distribution. Money, remember, costs nothing. If the bankers tried to resist, they would be sidetracked by the government which would issue money on its own account. And even if it escaped that danger the financial system would perish from want of good borrowers. For producers would soon be in possession of enough capital to finance their own developments."

"I see."

"Therefore the financial system will never part with fixed exchanges or with gold, which is the most convenient and most satisfactory 'peg' for these exchanges that has so far been devised. This golden 'peg' of the foreign exchanges is the lever whereby the price level in every country can be raised or lowered and whereby, therefore, the supply of good borrowers can be maintained."

The Home Minister rose and began to walk about the room.

"In theory, as you know," he went on, "the exchanges reflect the movements of goods and services. Exports pay for imports. If one exports more goods than one imports, one receives gold to make up the difference; if one imports more than one exports one pays gold out. And so on. Actually, however, as we have seen, it is possible by means of loans to foreigners to tip the balance one way or the other. The International Bankers, in other words, can create 'invisible imports' or 'invisible exports' by means of finance bills and other devices and so compel rapid and drastic changes in the price-levels and thus, also, in wage-levels. Think what the power means when one is dealing with a reluctant government. If the government in question refuses to grant the terms asked for, the International Bankers can put the exchanges against it, draw off its gold and compel it to cut wages and reduce public expenditure. Thus, the negotiating Government may find itself with a political crisis on its hands accompanied perhaps by strikes and riots."

The Home Minister approached the Bishop's desk and stood in front of it.

"So here is the process as it is now in operation. The International Banker lends promises to pay to those countries whose production is cheapest and where, therefore, the highest rates of interest are available. He lends these IOUs on the security of National incomes (bonds), of land (mortgages), of debentures and of cargoes of readily saleable commodities. By lending, he causes rises of bank rates in the countries from which the IOUs have been taken, each Home Banker being anxious to protect himself against a possible 'run' upon him if gold should begin to leave the country and if, in consequence, a sharp break in prices should occur. The rises in bank rates causes a falling off of borrowing and hence a gradual decline in buying power. Prices sag. Wages fall. Firms fail to pay the interest due on debentures and mortgages and Governments find themselves, owing to difficulty in collecting taxes, with unbalanced budgets. The market values of mortgages, debentures and Government bonds fall sharply. Bankers begin to sell the securities, the land and factories and workshops and even the government bonds against which they lend their IOUs. These securities naturally fetch very little and large amounts of them pass into the hands of the bankers themselves at 'rubbish' prices.

"The time has now come when the 'deflated' country is ripe for a new expansion of credit; for prices are low, wages are low and stocks are depleted. Back come the IOUs. Up go the prices. Soon the bankers are able to sell off the bonds, and land and factories and workshops and cargoes to new owners (or even to the old owners by means of loans from the bankers themselves) at a substantial profit. The sheep have been sheared. It is time to think about a new crop of wool."

"Terrible, terrible!"

The Bishop's voice was charged with a lively distress.

"And this," he said, "is the system of which I made myself the defender. You are quite right. The root of the evil is the lie that a man who has promised to pay ten times what he possesses can possibly fulfil his promises. The system, as you have shown me, marches from lie to lie - the lie that a loss of gold is disastrous, the lie that foreign exchanges must be kept fixed, the lie that a country lives by its export trade, the lie that purchasing power in the home market is an evil if it interferes with exports, the lie that high wages are a danger, the lie that a country which does not export more than it imports is living above its means, the lie that the remedy for over-production is economy in consumption. What a hideous pyramid of falsehood! And what a spectacle; a world glutted with goods on the one side and with hungry paupers on the other!"

The Bishop remained silent for a moment. Then he rose and stood facing his visitor.

"This system of IOUs," he asked, "was established, was it not, about the time that the power of the Christian Church in Europe began to weaken?"

"Yes. In the eighteenth century. The Christian Church absolutely forbade usury."

The old man nodded.

"I begin to see a war," he said, "of principalities and powers rather than of bankers and their victims."

He held out his hand to the Home Minister.

"I was an army chaplain," he said. "I saw so many men lay down their lives for what they believed to be righteousness. And so I lift up my heart. If the Christian civilization of Europe has not perished that is only because the spirit of its Founder dwells still in millions of hearts. Go out and tell the people. When that task has been accomplished fully, the fields will be white towards the harvest."

Notes and Quotes

First of all, the Quotes

"I am afraid the ordinary citizen will not like to be told that the banks can, and do, create money. The amount of money in existence varies only with the action of the banks in increasing and decreasing deposits and bank purchases. Every loan, overdraft or bank purchase creates a deposit and every repayment of a loan, overdraft or bank sale destroys a deposit. And they who control the credit of a nation direct the policy of Governments and hold in the hollow of their hands the destiny of the people."

The Rt. Hon. Reginald McKenna, Chairman of the Midland Bank at a meeting of the Midland Bank, January 1924.

"Today the nation returns to the noble metal, Gold."
The Rt. Hon. Winston Churchill, as Chancellor of the Exchequer, announcing the return to the Gold Standard in the House of Commons in April, 1925.

"Gold has been cornered, scrambled for, and hoarded. It has risen enormously in price, and the value of everything we have or earn has been diminished accordingly. This monstrous process has only to be continued long enough to shatter the civilisation, as it has already broken the prosperity, of the world as we have known it."

The Rt. Hon. Winston Churchill, speaking in the House of Commons on the evil effects of the Gold Standard. February 1932.

And now the Notes MOROTORIUM

When the First World War broke out in 1914, the Bank of England possessed only 9 million sterling in gold reserves and this sum constituted the effective legal tender reserve of all the banks in Great Britain.

The bank managers became seriously alarmed that the depositing public would demand their legal money. The public did demand gold coins in exchange for the banks' privately-issued notes, in many cases, and a run on the Bank of England followed.

After the nine million of gold sovereigns had been handed over the counters to the waiting crowds, in exchange for notes, the whole money system collapsed and it became necessary for the Government to declare a Bank Holiday, or Moratorium, for several days.

When the banks reopened, the public discovered that instead of getting their money back in gold, they were paid in a new legal tender of Treasury notes of £1 and 10/- [editor's note: 10/ - is ten shillings, or fifty pence in modern money].

This new legal tender currency amounting to £300,000,000 [editor's note: yes, three hundred million pounds as opposed to just nine million that has been held by the entire banking system in gold] had been issued by the State to the banks to save them from collapse. Had this new money not been issued, the private banking houses of Britain would have been compelled to default to their customers in a week's time.

CURRENCY

This means legal tender money whether notes or gold. This money is issued under the authority of Government.

CREDIT

This consists of the promises of bankers to pay currency. These promises-to-pay amount to about ten times the total of the currency. Credit is not legal tender money but, since it is used daily to buy goods and services and to pay debts, it performs the functions of money and is, in fact, indistinguishable from it.

Thus if the total was some £3,000,000,000 in use in this country:

£350,000,000 would be money issued by Government and £2,650,000,000 would consist of promises to pay issued by private individuals.

These promises to pay are issued only as loans repayable with interest. They can be withdrawn. So that the bankers actually have it in their power to remove nine-tenths of the buying power of the country whenever they choose to do so. Actually, of course, they content themselves with much smaller fluctuations of their credit because quite small fluctuations are enough to cause those changes in the level of prices, upwards or downwards, by which they live.

BANKERS

Bankers are lenders not of money but of promises to pay money. They lend promises-to-pay ten times the quantity of legal tender money which they possess. Consequently they live in permanent fear of "runs" upon them - that is to say of demands by the holders of their promises-to-pay for actual payment in legal tender money. The financial system is so designed as to reduce the danger of "runs" to the smallest possible dimensions.

A BANKER'S BALANCE SHEET

This shows how much legal tender money he possesses under the heading of "Cash and Deposits at the Central Bank".

The next item is always given as "Deposits" and these deposits are divided into "Advances" and "Securities". This means:

CASH

Legal tender money in the till and in the strong room.

DEPOSITS AT THE CENTRAL BANK

These are loans from the Central Bank given to private banks and secured by "collateral" - that is to say by government bonds, and other forms of high-class securities.

Deposits at the Central Bank count as cash in the sense that they can be changed immediately into legal tender money. The Central Bank, in other words, as the issuer, for the Government, of legal tender money, will always pay legal tender money on demand to those who have claims upon it. Private bankers therefore lend their clients promises-to-pay ten times the quantity of the deposits they, the private Bankers, possess at the Central Bank just as they lend promises-to-pay ten times the quantity of cash they possess. Cash and deposits at the Central Bank are really one and the same thing.

Nevertheless a difference between them does exist. Cash is cash. It is legal tender money. But, as has been said, deposits at the Central Bank are loans from the Central Bank. The Central Bank, like all banks, in other words, issues promises to pay legal tender money. It can, nevertheless, call up its loans and shorten sail like all other banks. It does this in several ways. The effect is to reduce every private bank's "deposits at the Central Bank" and so every private bank's holding of legal tender money.

When a private bank loses legal tender money it, too, has to shorten sail and call in its loans so that it may not, at any time, be lending promises-to-pay to a greater amount than ten times its holding of legal tender money. For example:

A private bank has:

Cash	£100
Deposits at the Central Bank	£100
	=====
Total	£200

It will lend promises-to-pay to the amount of £2,000.

But the Central Bank now calls up £50 of its loan, and so the private bank has:

Cash	£100
Deposits at the Central Bank	£ 50
	===
Total	£150

The private bank will now lend promises-to-pay to the amount only of £1,500.

Thus the system by which private banks borrow from the Central Bank enables the Central Bank to control them by increasing or decreasing the amounts of their legal tender money.

But the Central Bank itself is controlled by the movements of gold because, when the gold standard is working, it is compelled to withdraw notes to the full value of any gold which it may be exporting from the country. An export of gold, therefore, causes the Central Bank to "retire" notes and this may force it to reduce its loans ("deposits at the Central Bank") to the private banks.

Movements of gold are determined by the relationship existing between exports and imports. If exports do not pay for imports gold will leave the country to settle the bill. If exports exceed imports gold will come into the country to settle to bill. But it is possible for international bankers to "tip" this balance of exports and imports by making loans across the exchanges in such a way that gold may be demanded by the borrowers of the money. The International Bankers, therefore, really do control the movements of gold.

And so we have:

Employment and profits depend on the price level. The price level depends on the quantity of money.

The quantity of money depends on private bankers' loans.

Private bankers' loans depend on Deposits at the Central Bank. Deposits at the Central Bank depend on Central Bank loans.

Central Bank loans depend on movements of gold. Movements of gold depend on the Foreign Exchanges.

The Foreign Exchanges can be made to depend on

the operations of International Finance.

Consequently the old nursery rhyme can be applied with accuracy thus:

"The International Banker began to lend his promises-to-pay across the Exchanges. His promises-to-pay began to lead to an export of gold. The export of gold began to make the Central Bank call in its loans. The calling in of the Central Bank's loans began to make the private bankers call in their loans. The calling in of the private bankers' loans began to cause prices to fall. The fall in prices began to cause a fall in profits. The fall in profits began to cause a fall in wages and unemployment. And then the country produced more cheaply and the International Banker didn't have to honour his promises-to-pay by giving money for them after all.

And so he got 8 per cent in a far country without having to part with a penny piece. Which was as well, seeing that he possessed no money."

DEPOSITS

It is important to distinguish between:

"Deposits at the Central Bank" and "Deposits". The former are loans to the private banker, the latter are loans made by him.

Deposits, in fact, mean loans of promises to pay legal tender. Deposits therefore amount as a rule to ten times the private bankers' holding of "Cash and

Deposits at the Central Bank".

ADVANCES

Private bankers divide their deposits into "Advances" and "Securities". Advances are loans of promises-to-pay industrialists, farmers, manufacturers and so on. They are, therefore, money in the market. When a private banker is taking in sail it is his advances which will shrink.

SECURITIES

When private bankers do not wish to lend their promises-to-pay to producers they buy securities, for example War Loan, with them. Thus in times of boom "advances" are increased; in times of slump an increase in "securities" takes place. This merely means that, when trade is bad, bankers like to have the government itself for their borrower. Hence the cry that governments must balance their budget.

LOANS TO THE MONEY MARKET

Private bankers always lend some of their promises to the Money Market, that is to say, to the International Bankers. These are short term loans, and hence readily available in case of need. Thus a private banker might have:

Cash and Deposits at the Central Bank   £10
Deposits:

Loans to Money Market   £10

Advances	£50
Securities (Government and other)	£30
Total Deposits	£100

PRICE LEVEL

If the price level falls all debts become more burdensome because it takes more goods to pay them off. If a farmer can pay his rent with two sheep he is obviously better off than when it requires four sheep to pay the same rent.

A rise in the price level reduces the burden of debt by reducing the quantity of goods needed to pay off debts.

FOREIGN EXCHANGE MARKET

The market where promises to pay, e.g. pounds, are sold for promises to pay, e.g. dollars, francs and so on. The value of every such promise-to-pay is determined by the demand for it. If there is a big demand for promises to pay pounds by holders of promises to pay dollars, the dollar will fall in relation to the pound. In other words more dollars will be needed to buy a pound than formerly. This is what happens when exchanges are "unpegged".

Pegging a currency means that it is prevented from falling by an export of gold. If owners of promises to pay dollars, for example, are able to change their promises into gold, they will do so if dollars look like losing their value; for gold, having a fixed price everywhere, cannot lose its value. If, for example, the owner of a promise to pay five dollars can no longer get a pound for his promises to pay he will change his promises into gold by demanding their fulfilment. The gold he obtains from the banker making the promises will buy rather more than a pound. Gold as a result of this transaction will leave America to come to England. When it leaves America a corresponding quantity of dollar notes will be withdrawn from circulation and American prices, therefore, will be made to fall.

When the gold reaches England a corresponding quantity of pound notes will be put into circulation and English prices, therefore, will be made to rise. Thus America will be better able to export goods than England and so the demand for dollars (to pay for the exported goods) will increase and the demand for pounds will fall. Dollar and pound will now once more be level with one another and the bankers issuing promises to pay dollars will no longer be asked to redeem these promises.

DISCOUNT MARKET

Market where promises-to-pay of various bankers are borrowed on short terms by Government (on security of Treasury bills), by international bankers (on security of finance bills) and by traders and merchants (on security of commercial bills).

The Discount Market and the Foreign Exchange Market are necessarily closely related. Thus bill brokers, bullion brokers, discount houses, acceptance houses, private banks and the Central Bank itself have a common meeting ground in what is generally called The Money Market.

Examples of Central Banks are the Bank of England, the Banque de France, the Reichsbank, and the Federal Reserve System. These are often called "bankers' banks". Practice varies from country to country but the bed-rock principles do not vary.